TOP CANADIAN
CONTEMPORARY ARCHITECTS

Edited by Zhang Yuhua   Planned by Archiwisdom Book   Translated by Lin Xi

TOP CANADIAN CONTEMPORARY ARCHITECTS

Copyright © 2012 by ifengspace Culture & Media Co., Ltd.

Published by Phoenix Publishing Limited

Room 510-511D2, Nam Fung Tower, 173 Des Voeux Road Central, Hong Kong, China

E-mail: info@ phoenix-book.com

http://www.phoenix-book.com

Distributed by Phoenix Publishing Limited.

E-mail: sales@ phoenix-book.com

ISBN: 978-988-15903-9-8
Printed in China
First Print 2012.4

This book collects nearly 50 architecture projects from Canadian architects. The collected projects with different styles and unique design are the Canadian top architects' latest masterpieces. The book includes four sections: culture, commerce, residence and office. Each section has 5 to 20 projects. Every project is presented with design interpretation both in English and Chinese, real photos, plans, elevation drawings and some engineering drawings. With a high reference value, it represents the main architectural style, as well as excellent design levels of architect in the world.

This book is planned by Archiwisdom Book Studio. It serves as the valuable reference in the field of architecture practice and also one of the significant high-end readings reflecting the trends of public architecture design.

FOREWORD

CONTENTS

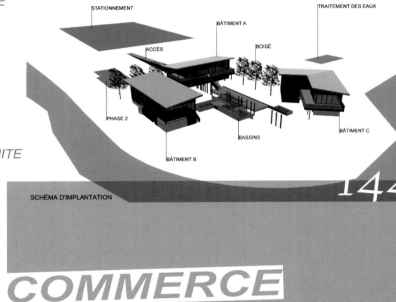

STATIONNEMENT   BÂTIMENT A   TRAITEMENT DES EAUX   ACCÈS   BOISÉ   PHASE 2   BASSINS   BÂTIMENT C   BÂTIMENT B

SCHÉMA D'IMPLANTATION

144

COMMERCE

6

CULTURE

RESIDENCE
208

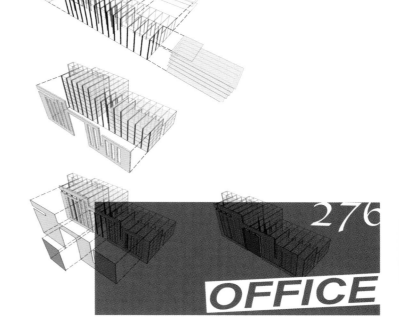

276

OFFICE

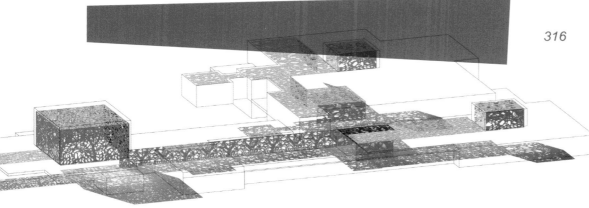

CULTURE

Architects: Briere, Gilbert + Associates, Architecture & Design Urbain

Location: Boucherville, Quebec, Canada

Photographer: Christian Perreault

MONTARVILLE — BOUCHER DE LA BRUÈRE PUBLIC LIBRARY

Montarville - Boucher de la Bruère Public Library is located in the downtown core of Boucherville, situated on the banks of the St. Lawrence River just east of the Island of Montreal. With a long histry of almost 30 years, the municipal library needs to expand and reconfigure its existing facilities so that it can better pursue its mission and provide services in accordance with new and emerging social, cultural and technological trends.

This project, which was the award winner in a 2007 architectural competition, consists of a three-storey expansion (1,470 m²) plus a refit of the existing structure (1,700 m²). It includes an atrium, a new entrance hall, a new library promenade, a new loans counter and a complete reorganization of all the library collections.

In contrast to the existing building, whose introverted geometry suggests only the slightest relationship with its immediate social and natural environment, the approach adopts an open,

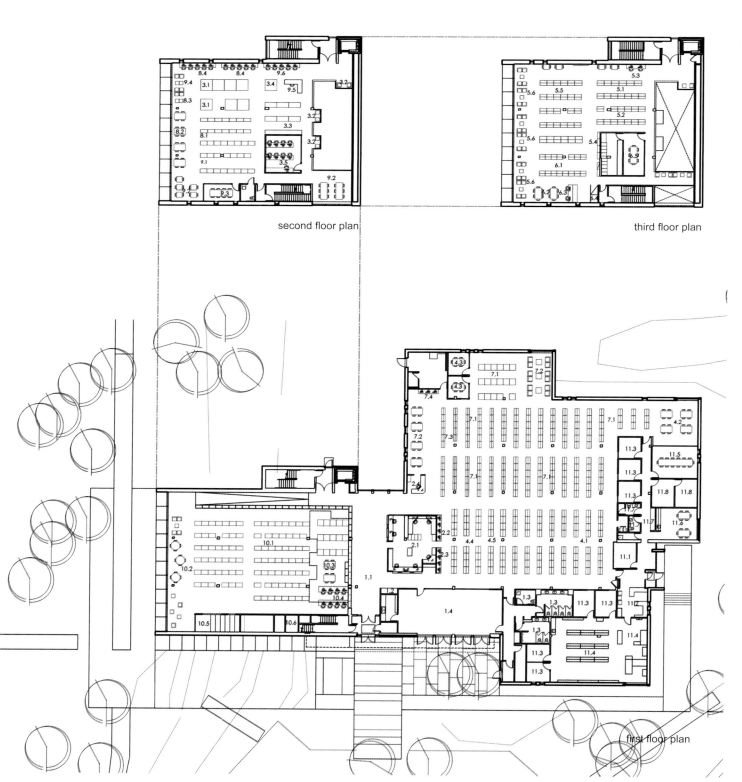

second floor plan

third floor plan

first floor plan

10

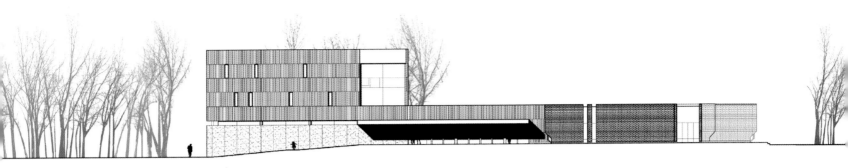

south elevation

barrier-free design that will convey the very essence of a centre whose essential function is discovery, as well as openness to knowledge and to the world.

The expansion is simple, open and effective, to the benefit of all library patrons. Like a unifying link, it pulls together the component parts, giving concrete expression to the new physical and visual elements that connect the library to its urban context and the Rivière aux Pins Park. A new promenade serves as the path to the Rivière aux Pins Park,

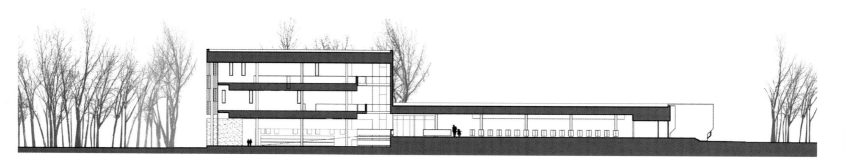

longitudinal section

enabling the library to be bathed in the nature, which is also the stimulus for the conceptual approach and further development of that idea.

The three storeys are home to the library's three general collections – books for children, adolescents and adults. Taking advantage of the natural topography of the site and of the proximity of the trees, a large three-storey glass wall allows for diverse visual links between the indoor spaces and the woods. Consequently, each clientele

(children, adolescents, adults and senior citizens) benefits from a distinct relationship with the vegetation, the trees and the foliage, which inspire calm, silence and rejuvenation.

Directly linked to existing footpaths, the new promenade runs alongside the building. It follows the contours of the topography and directs visitors toward the new reception area and main entrance, thereby anchoring the library to its immediate context, its neighbourhood and its town.

WINNERS OF THE CAHP AWARDS PAR

Fournier Gersovitz Moss & Associates Architects (FGMAA) is proud to announce that it has received two awards for preservation of a heritage building under the most recent Canadian Association of Heritage Professionals (CAHP) Awards Program. FGMAA received an award of merit for the restoration of the F.A.C.E School's auditorium in Montreal, and an award for restoration of the West Block Building and Southeast Tower on Parliament

Hill in Ottawa.

F.A.C.E School's auditorium in Montreal

Located in a Neo-Classical building constructed in 1914, F.A.C.E (Formation Artistique au Coeur de l'Éducation) is a public, bilingual nursery, primary, and secondary school. It was founded in 1975 to offer an alternative education program combining

conventional studies and art curricula. FGMAA was mandated by the Montreal school board to restore the school's auditorium and redefine its use in the context of a changing academic curriculum. The purpose of rehabilitation of the auditorium was to both restore its original splendor and update its equipment.

West Block Building and Southeast Tower on Parliament Hill in Ottawa

In 1995, FGMAA, in association with the Arcop Group of Montreal, received the mandate to rehabilitate the West Block Building on Parliament Hill in Ottawa. The project includes the complete rehabilitation of the building and the construction of an interim House of Commons in view of the renovation of the Centre Block. Public Works Canada decided to proceed with consolidation of the Southeast Tower of the building, and to make a benchmark project for continuation of the restoration of the building's exterior. Because of the serious degradation of the tower's walls, implementation of the project necessitated the design and erection of an independent freestanding scaffolding system.

The team of architects at FGMAA proved their professionalism, efficiency, and vast experience in preservation of heritage buildings by completing these two projects with excellence and within the planned deadlines and budgets.

Architects: Provencher Roy, Associates Architects

Location: Montreal, Quebec, Canada

MONTREAL MUSEUM OF FINE ARTS

Montreal Museum of Fine Arts, which celebrated its 150th anniversary in 2010, is expanding,adding the fourth pavilion on the base of the three, according to the the decisions of the board of directors. The addition of this fourth pavilion will more than double the area devoted to Quebec and Canadian art. The museum will soon be presenting a unique and coherent look at the history of Quebec and Canadian art. With admission and audioguides free of charge at all times, it will give thousands of visitors, school groups, families and tourists an opportunity to learn more about the heritage, which will be shown here in a historical context.

450 professionals and craftsmen convene on this huge building to combine the museum function with a church built in the late nineteenth century. Not only is the museum's function an ideal fit with the church, giving it a new life, it also makes it possible to conserve a "Canadian architectural treasure", with plenty of comporary fragrance. Its exceptional integration of conventional and urban design, brings past and future together. What's more, the Bourgie Concert Hall into the museum will present numerous concerts and activities every year, helping spark a new, perfect dialogue between the visual arts and music.

Architect: Daoust Lestage Inc. Architecture Design Urbain

Engineer: Dessau Ingénierie Inc.

Location: Montreal, Quebec, Canada

Site Area: 11, 853 m²

Built Area: 8,175m²

Photographers: Marc Carmer, Daoust Lestage (Marie-Josée Gagnon)

CARTIERVILLE Y CENTRE — A COMMUNITY BEACON

The Cartlerville Y Centre is a pavilion glowing through a screen of vegetation. Located in an economically depressed neighborhood; the building becomes a beacon in the urban landscape. By day, the white concrete block facade is a festive marker on a park-like site. At night, the signature lighting and large glazed openings invite the community to take part in civic and athletic activities.

The building splits into two volumes each connected to distinctly oriented North and South urban fabric, thus creating a delaminated central spine. The North and South wings become two level, inhabited sports plateaus housing the fitness centre, swimming pool, track and multi-functional rooms, respectively.

The entrance lobby, and main circulation space, is the connector of the north-south volumes, forming an interior pedestrian street. The entrance lobby and interior space are connected and split by a series of French windows, creating a strong sense of transparency and visual continuity from floor to floor and indoor to outdoor.

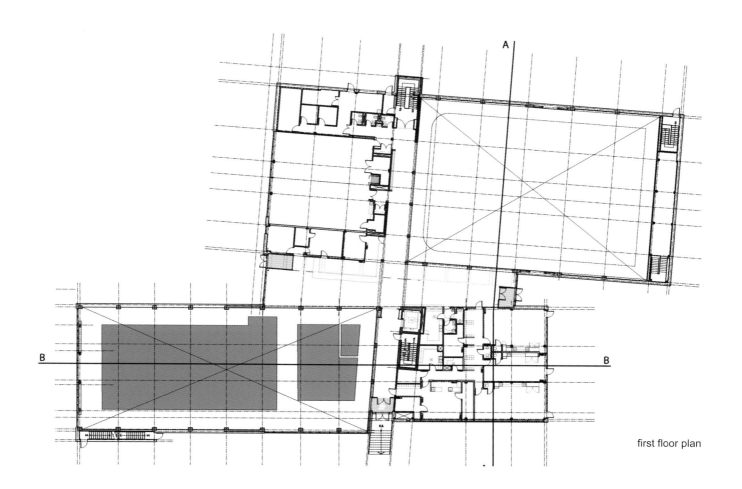

first floor plan

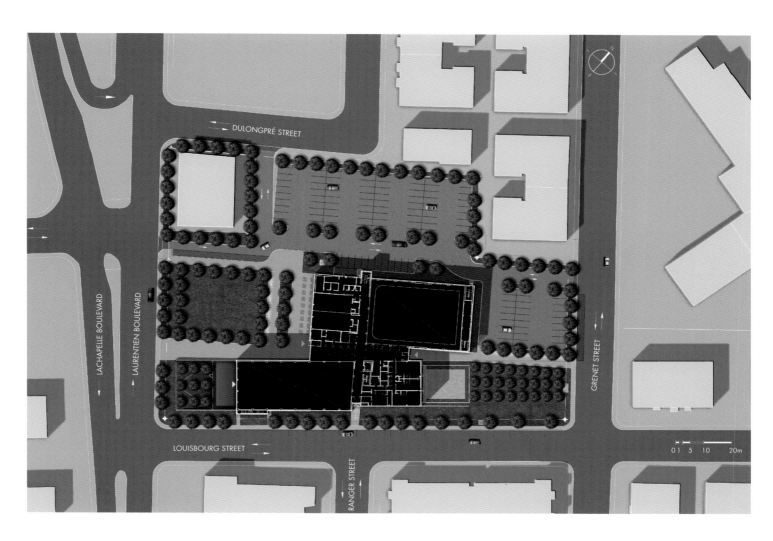

DULONGPRÉ STREET

LACHAPELLE BOULEVARD

LAURENTIEN BOULEVARD

GRENET STREET

LOUISBOURG STREET

RANGER STREET

0 1   5   10   20m

On the lower level of the southern volume, the pool deck extends West to the level of the street. To the north, the track surrounding the upper perimeter of the gym projects the runner into nature.

From the urban gestures to the architectural resolution, the Cartlerville Y Centre is designed with a holistic approach to sustainability. In combination with the white facade and white roofing membrane the heat island effect is reduced and a geothermal system completes the sustainable strategy.

The architecture also strives to foster sustainable communities. The transparent facade invites the public to become a part of the community and of the centre. On the upper level, the fitness centre, swimming pool, track and multi-functional rooms are arranged on either side of the building's spine. These spaces benefit from open views to each other as well as elevated views towards the lobby, pool and gym below showcasing community life. As a result of the generous transparency of the spaces, both inwards and outwards, the Cartlerville Y Centre projects a genuine desire for openness to the community.

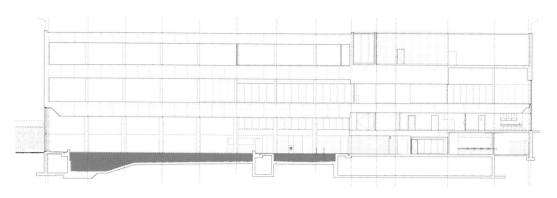

section BB

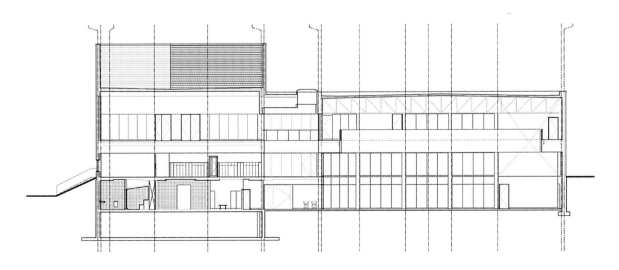

section AA

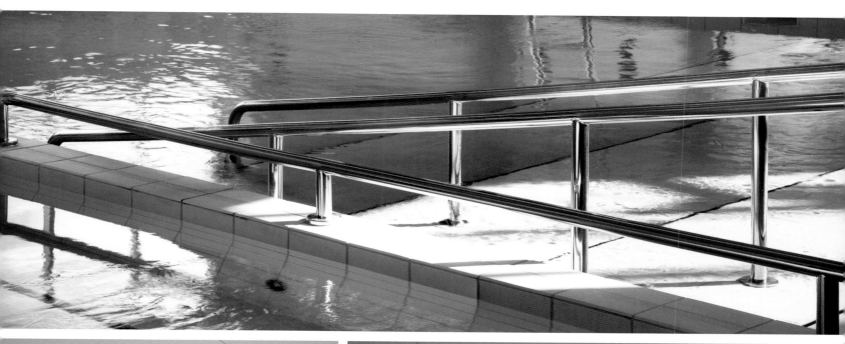

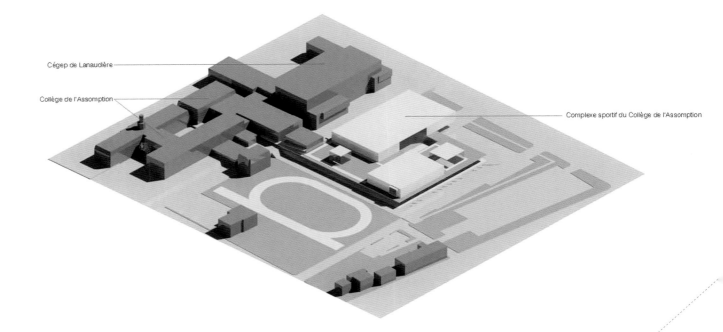

Cégep de Lanaudière

Collège de l'Assomption

Complexe sportif du Collège de l'Assomption

COMPLEXE SPORTIF DE L'ASSOMPTION

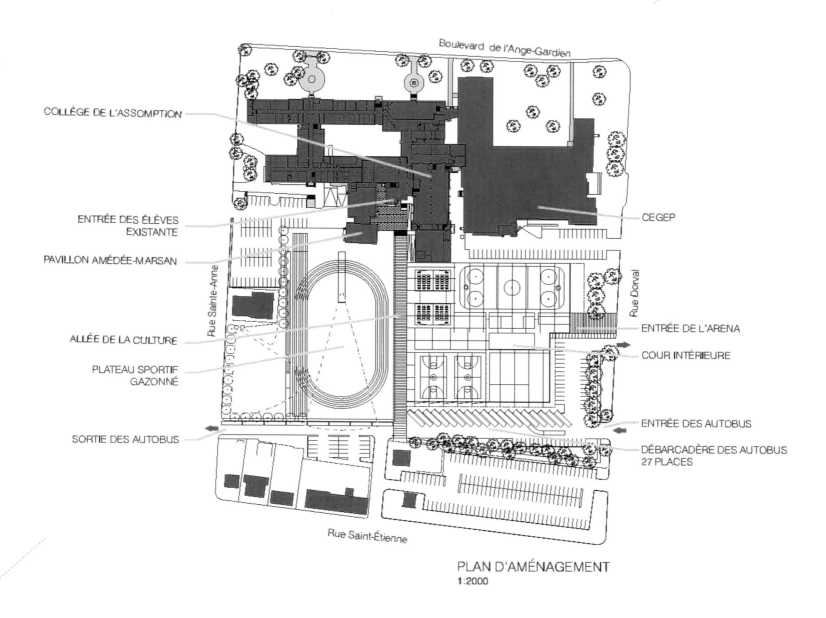

COLLÈGE DE L'ASSOMPTION

Boulevard de l'Ange-Gardien

CEGEP

ENTRÉE DES ÉLÈVES EXISTANTE

PAVILLON AMÉDÉE-MARSAN

Rue Sainte-Anne

Rue Dorval

ALLÉE DE LA CULTURE

ENTRÉE DE L'ARENA

COUR INTÉRIEURE

PLATEAU SPORTIF GAZONNÉ

ENTRÉE DES AUTOBUS

SORTIE DES AUTOBUS

DÉBARCADÈRE DES AUTOBUS 27 PLACES

Rue Saint-Étienne

PLAN D'AMÉNAGEMENT
1:2000

L'Assomption College is a private high school founded in 1884 in a small town near Montreal. This college, that hosts 1,250 students, has become the heart of the social, cultural and sportive life of the Lanaudière region. The project aims at efficiently waking use of college space and providing functional infrastructure.

The crumbling municipal hockey arena that was also built alongside the college needed to be replaced. It led to the decision to build a new sport center including a double gymnasium, workout and dance rehearsal rooms and a new ice rink.

The existing hockey arena was demolished to reorganize the site, clearing a large space for a new football field and race track along the sport centre. It also cleared views on the existing Amédée-

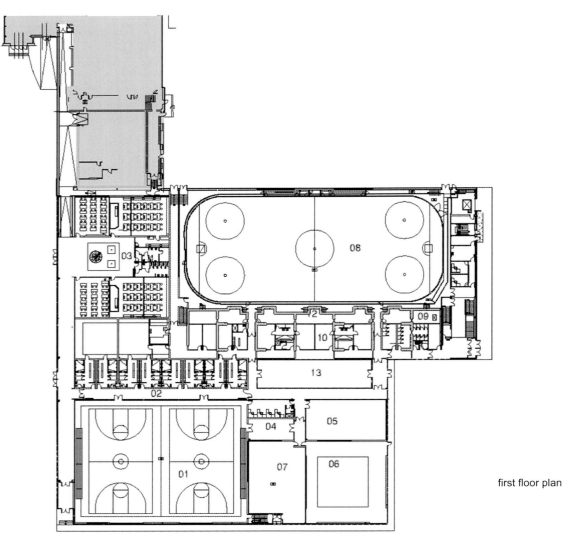

first floor plan

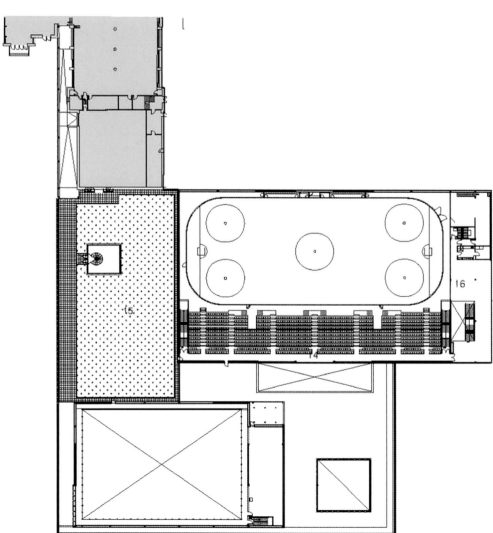

second floor plan

Marsan pavillion, gave a distinctive entrance to the new arena allowing that it operates independently and helped reorganize the students arrivals and departures area that was originally chaotic.

The formal strategy used in this project takes advantage of the level difference between the ground floor of the existing college and the construction site to establish a continuous horizontal datum at mid height between these two levels all along the perimeter of the new building. The lower half is largely glassed while the volumes of the arena and gymnasium, the glass box of the green roof access and the dance rehearsal room emerge above this base. The roof which is at the same level as the ground floor of the existing college gives a privileged point of view to watch events taking place on the sport field.

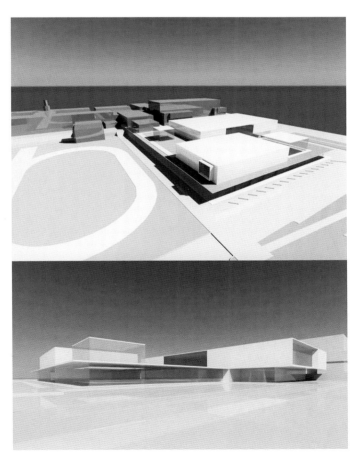

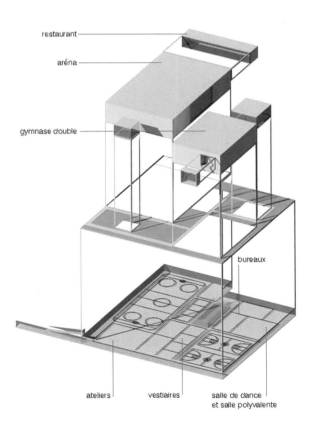

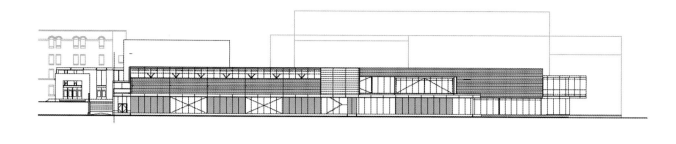

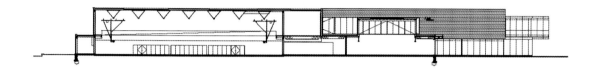

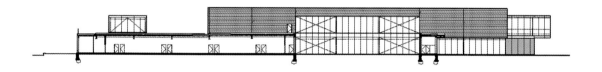

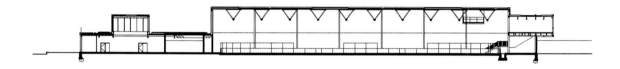

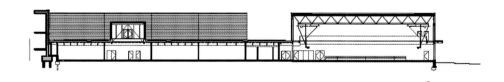

41

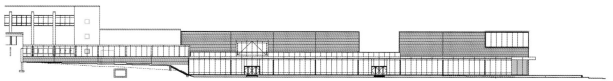

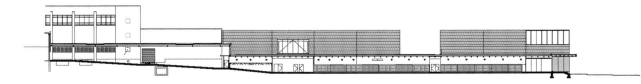

Architect: Saia Barbarese Topouzanov Architects

Photographers: Marc Cramer, Frédéric Saia, Vladimir Topouzanov

EXPANSION OF SPORTIF J.-C. MALÉPART CENTRE

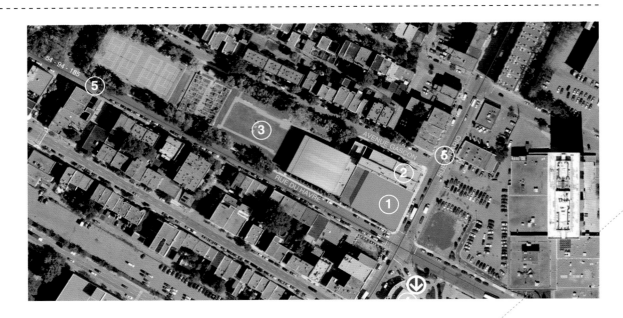

The new building had to complement the surrounding urban fabric and form a unit with the articulated volumes of the 1996 sports centre.

The project has creatively applied the idea of waves. Both indoors and outdoors, a wave develops on the perimeter of the building, rising and falling in two continuous undulations. The first, transparent and high opposite to the entrance and the training room, surges as far as the corner near the diving board, providing an ambience propitious to concentration. Then the glass rises along the wading pool and reflects the green world outside, conveying the idea of "healthy sports"

The dialogue between the new building and the old one is natural The grey-tinted glass harmonizes with the colors of the earlier structure. It gives passers-by an idea of what is going on inside while preserving some privacy for users. The milky tone and reflective quality of the upper wall are echoed in the material for the roof to ensure the extension from one to the other in contrast with the clear demarcations of the building.

first floor plan

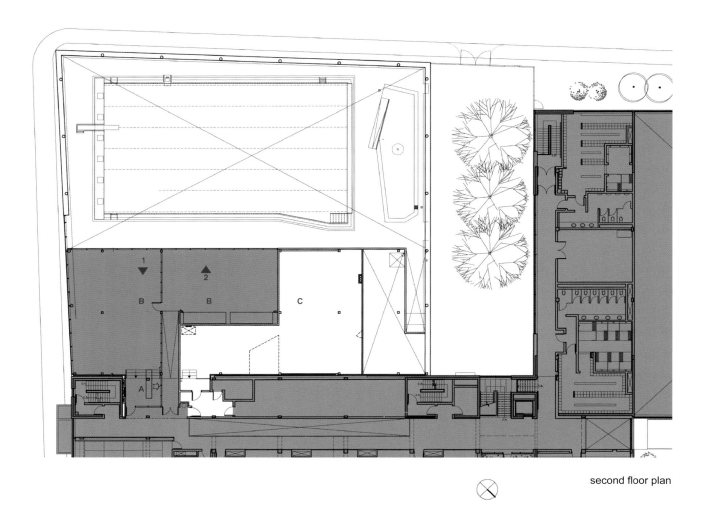

second floor plan

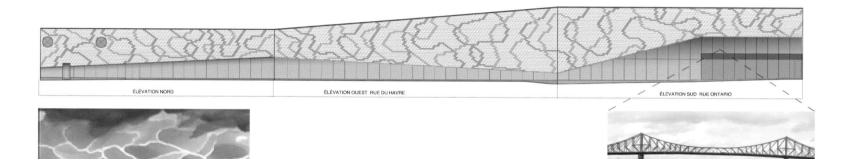

ÉLÉVATION NORD   ÉLÉVATION OUEST RUE DU HAVRE   ÉLÉVATION SUD RUE ONTARIO

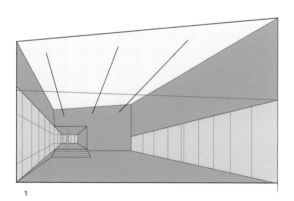

1

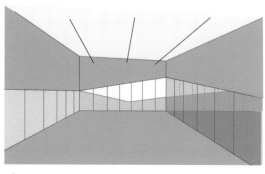

2

This architectural project is, above all, people-oriented. It is respectful of passers-by, who find themselves walking beside a shimmering wall beyond which they can divine movement inside, and the entrance beckons like an invitation. The project is even more concerned with the well-being and health of users, encouraging passers-by to develop healthy lifestyle. The construction process, the systems implemented, and the air and water recycling were all designed with sustainable development in mind. All of these concerns modulate an architectural language in step with current ideas, locally and internationally, that the pursuit of the healthy, high-quality life has already come into being, not a dream.

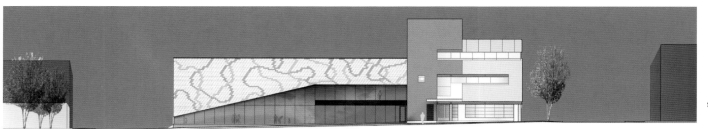

south elevation

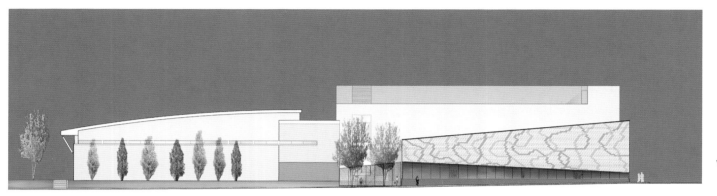

west elevation

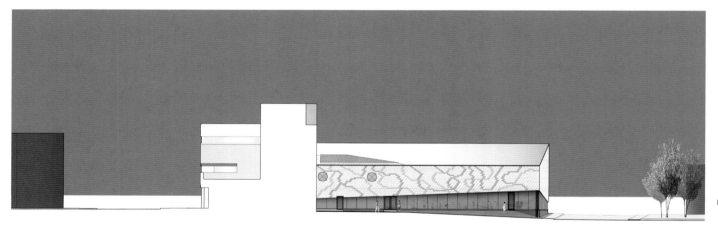

north elevation

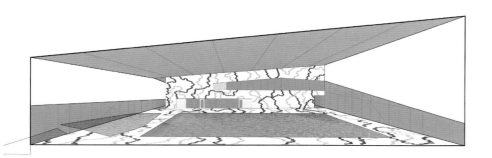

1

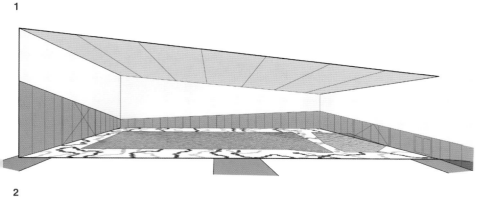

2

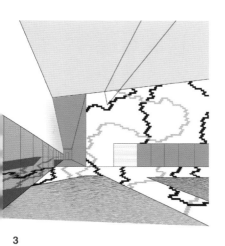

3

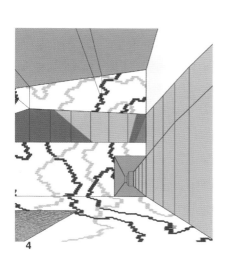

4

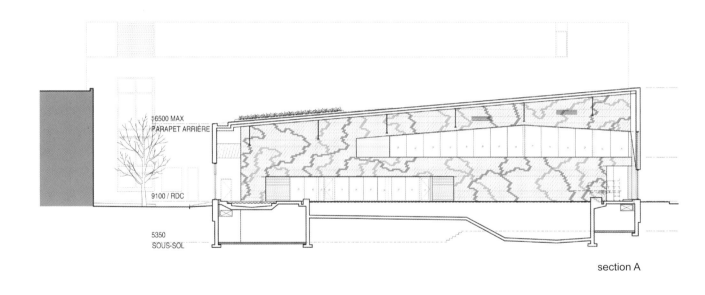

16500 MAX
PARAPET ARRIÈRE

9100 / RDC

5350
SOUS-SOL

section A

A

B

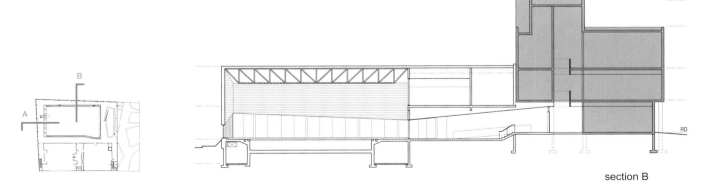

RD

section B

53

PIERREFONDS COMMUNAUTAIRE CENTRE

The Pierrefonds-Roxboro borough located on the west end of Montréal's island contains a population of more than 65,000 inhabitants. It has an excellent location. The proximity of a train station, a school, a youth centre and a park led the municipal authorities to implement a new community center facilitating the integration of new citizens with the help of social organizations and volunteers.

To avoid institutional stigmatization, the project adopts the morphology of commercial buildings: one-storey building with large fenestration and a overhanging roof on small columns.

This voluntary simplicity enabled us to provide the project with a green roof, an outdoor bandstand. The green roof serves as a perfect protection from the heavy sunshine in summer and standing on the bandstand, it is pleasant to sing a song.

A cladding of silicon coated glass panels and a glossy powder coating on aluminium plates were chosen for their resistance to graffiti, also ensuring that it is full of natural country fragrance.

The centre includes a multipurpose room for 150 persons, classrooms of different sizes and a communal kitchen, which is beautiful and highly functional.

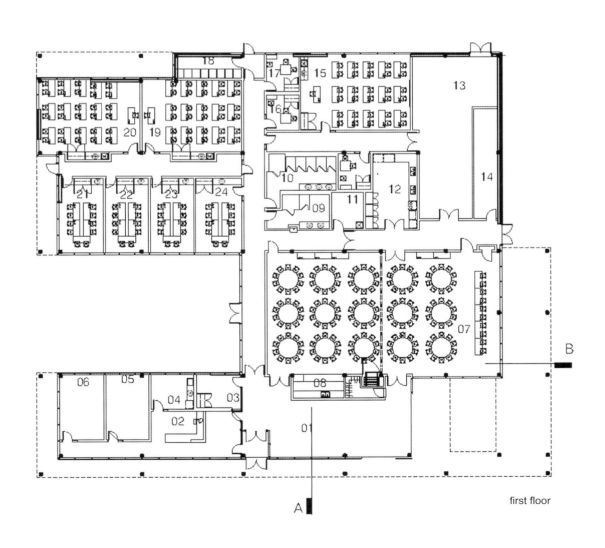

first floor

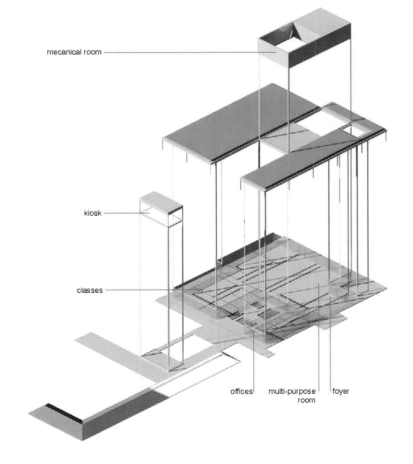

mecanical room

kiosk

classes

offices   multi-purpose   foyer
           room

59

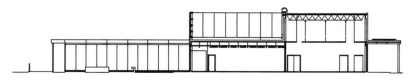

section A

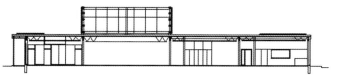

section B

elevations

Architect: Saia Barbarese Topouzanov Architects

Area: 4,560 m²

DENISE PELLETIER — GRANADA THEATRE

Granada Theatre, built in 1930, is situated in the former municipality of Maisonneuve, at the northwest corner of Boulevard Morgan and Rue Sainte-Catherine. In the vicinity, prestigious buildings such as C. L. Dufort's City Hall, as well as the Maisonneuve Market and Maisonneuve Baths, both by M. Dufresne, testified to the city's prosperity and its architects' talents in the early twentieth century. The Beaux-Arts style then in fashion borrowed columns, arcades, and motifs from Antiquity or the Renaissance. In line with this trend, the Granada was among the wave of North American movie theatres that looked like palaces, with chandeliers, drapes, loges, gold-leaf paint, faux-marble finishes, and more.

Intending to refine a "Spanish atmospheric design," developers asked architect Emmanuel Briffa to take over the Granada project Briffa, an experienced decorator, had designed numerous theatres in eastern Canada, almost twenty of them in Montreal and Quebec City.

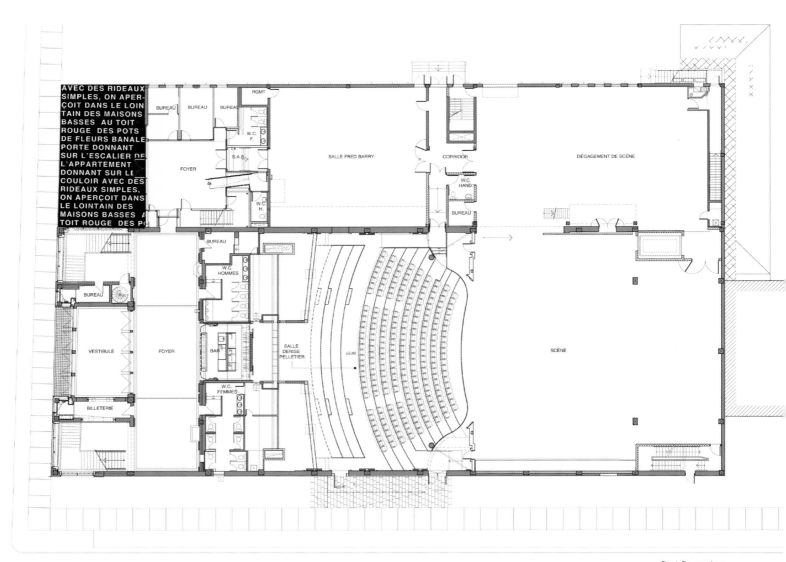

AVEC DES RIDEAUX
SIMPLES, ON APER-
ÇOIT DANS LE LOIN-
TAIN DES MAISONS
BASSES AU TOIT
ROUGE DES POTS
DE FLEURS BANALE
PORTE DONNANT
SUR L'ESCALIER DE
L'APPARTEMENT
DONNANT SUR LE
COULOIR AVEC DES
RIDEAUX SIMPLES,
ON APERÇOIT DANS
LE LOINTAIN DES
MAISONS BASSES A
TOIT ROUGE DES PC

first floor plan

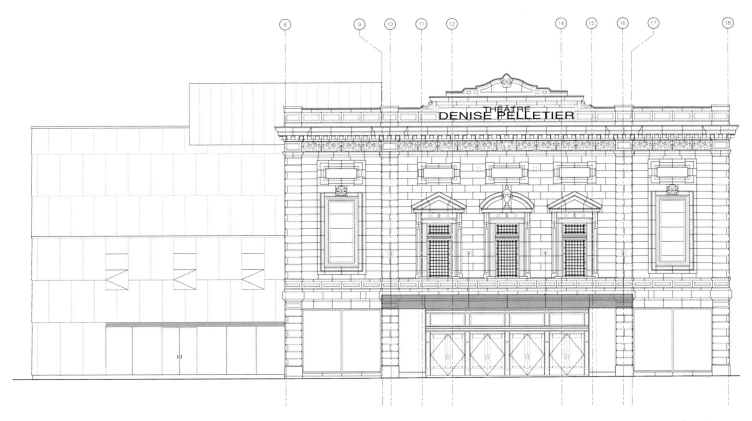

elevations

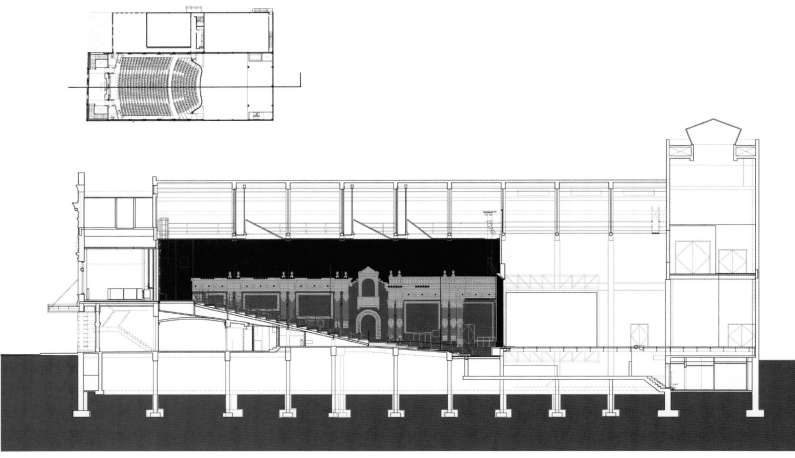

section

In the original building, the tone was set the moment one set eyes on the theatre. The front façade had an elaborately patterned cladding of prefabricated, beige-tinted stones. The basic rectangular shape was crowned with a cornice with modillions, a frieze, and a small pediment featuring the theatre's name, "Granada." Horizontally, the façade was subdivided into two registers. The ground floor offered a wide opening with central doors sheltered by a light wrought-work marquee, flanked by display windows. The upper floor, taller than the ground floor, extended the tripartite vertical subdivision. In the centre, three Renaissance-style windows rise above the entrance. The rest of the building is clad in brick, with simple lines and easy procedures.

The luxurious interior matched the exterior. From a rather plain vestibule, visitors enter the lobby. The drop-arch moldings of the coffered ceiling sit on the brackets. The lobby features a fireplace and a fountain, like a beautiful picturesque, with a strong sense of visual impact.

Granada Theatre serves as a visual feast of luxurious design and elegant art fragrance. It deserves the classical model in the field of theatre architecture, with dynamic vibrancy and forever warmth.

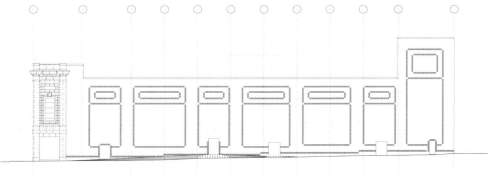

east elevation

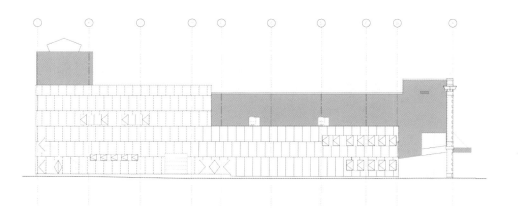

west elevation

68

Architect: KPMB

Location: Toronto, Ontario, Canada

GARDINER MUSEUM OF CERAMIC ART

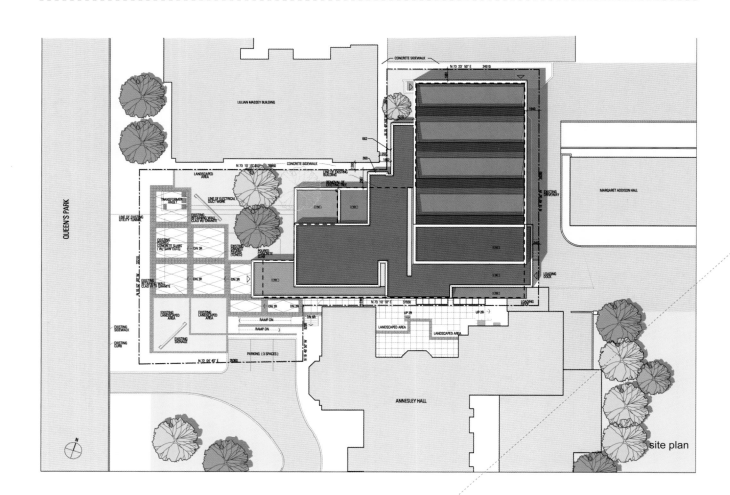

site plan

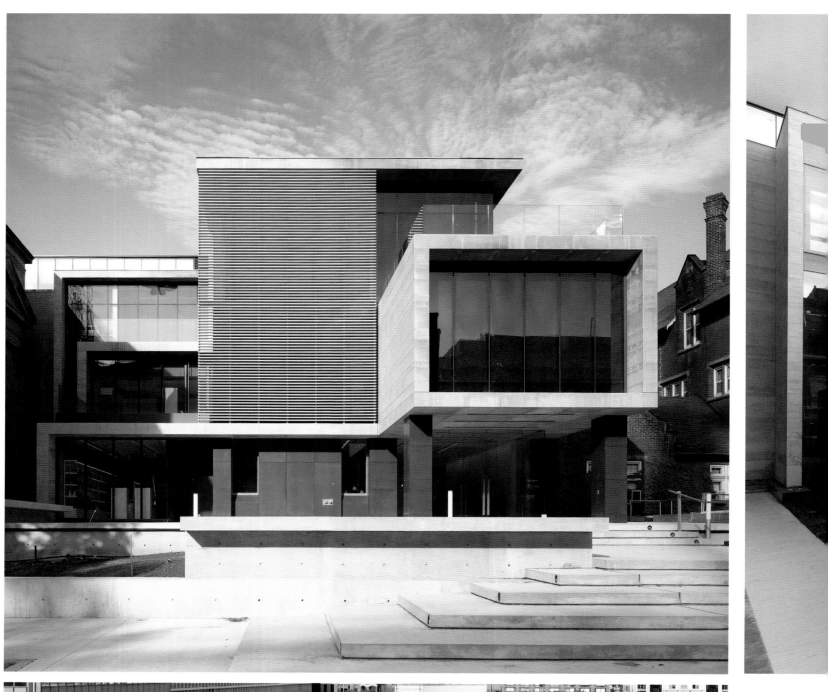

Gardiner Museum of Ceramic Art is one of the world's pre-eminent institutions devotedto ceramic art, and the only museum of its kind in Canada. It is also one of the major projects in Toronto's cultural renaissance. The Gardiner renewal, together with the Royal Ontario Museum across the street and the Royal Conservatory of Music around the corner on Bloor Street West, will form a new cultural precinct for the city.

Framed between the neoclassical Lillian Massey building to the north and the Queen Anne-style Margaret Addison Hall to the south, it has an excellent location.

The addition of approximately 1,300 m^2 creates a new contemporary gallery to host international exhibits of large-scale contemporary works, provides much-needed storage for the expanding permanent collection, and incorporates new studio and curatorial facilities to support the Gardiner's popular community-outreach programs and its research activities. The design also greatly enhances the museum's revenue-generating potential with a larger, more accessible retail shop, a rentable multi-purpose event space, and a destination restaurant.

GARDINER   10.05.01

The renewal builds on top of the original structure, designed by Keith Wagland in 1984, to anticipate vertical expansion. The original pink granite exterior is replaced with polished buff limestone to give the Gardiner a more contemporary image. The limestone seamlessly weaves existing and expanded spaces together. The front of the museum is completely re-landscaped with a series of terraced platforms that provide a gradual ascent into the forecourt of the building.

A cubic volume marks the entrance to the building. During the day, the cube's broad expanse of floor-to-ceiling glazing creates a reflective surface which mirrors

the outside street, and at night, acts as a window into the museum's activities. This column-free area with a clerestorey ceiling creates a monumental space for large-scale contemporary and traveling exhibits.

The retail store and restaurant are on the corner of the museum, providing exquisite souvenirsand a delicious feast.

The design emphasizes a subtle interplay between transparency and lightness, The consistent language of materials, custom-designed casework, and precise detailing provide a miracle in the field of contemporary art architecture.

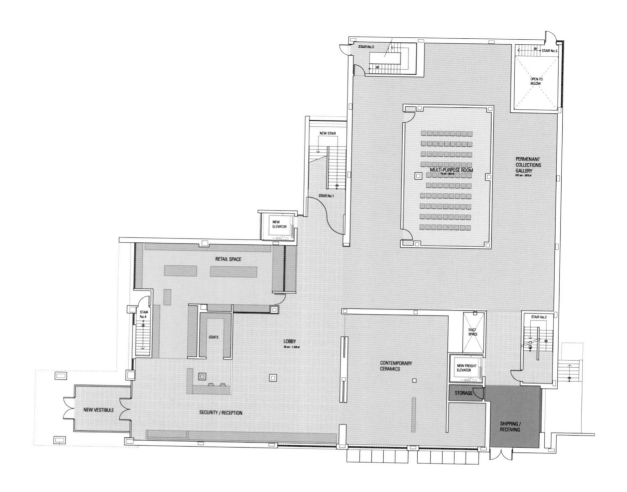

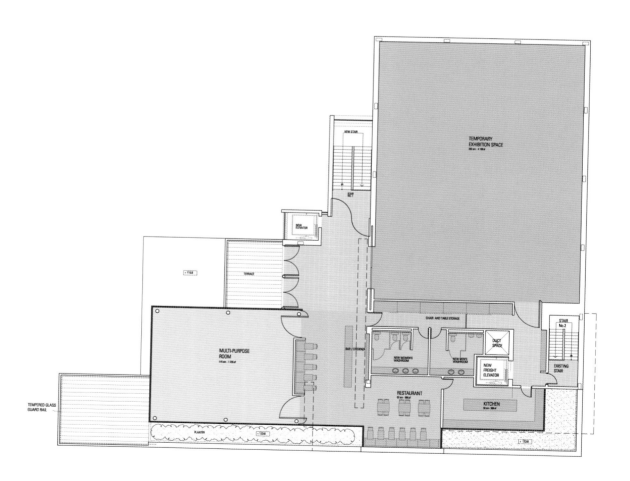

Architects: Menkès Shooner Dagenais, LeTourneux Architects

Artist: Yechel Gagnon

Location: Montreal, Quebec, Canada

Photographers: Marc Cramer, Alexandre Masino, Pierre Charrier

JEAN-DE-BRÉBEUF COLLEGE — PUBLIC ART

The project aims to create a novel space for the Jean-De-Brébeuf College.

The space offered at the college, through the long corridor and the grand foyer, is double and unique; double in its dimensions and functions, unique by its majestic architecture that embraces the exterior garden and its natural elements. The designers thus chose to use the two different techniques that may be seen here, frottage drawing and carved plywood.

Frottage drawing serves as a kind of brand-new drawing technology created by displacement of the paper. It presents an imagery oscillating between abstraction and an imaginary landscape echoing a certain tradition of Chinese ink painting.

Carved plywood, consisting of different formats, presents various vertical architectural lines of the wall. They accentuate the rhythm in symbiosis with the architecture. Wood, an organic element, crosses the transparency of the window to rejoin the beauty of the exterior garden, which is full inspiration.

The convergence of frottage drawing, carved plywood and garden with inspirable scents, will have the pleasure to find themselves in presence of a single work of art, like a beautiful, harmonious song.

It is a marvelous college space, providing memorable enjoy.

ENTRY FOR THE COMPETITION FOR THE SAINT-LAURENT LIBRARY

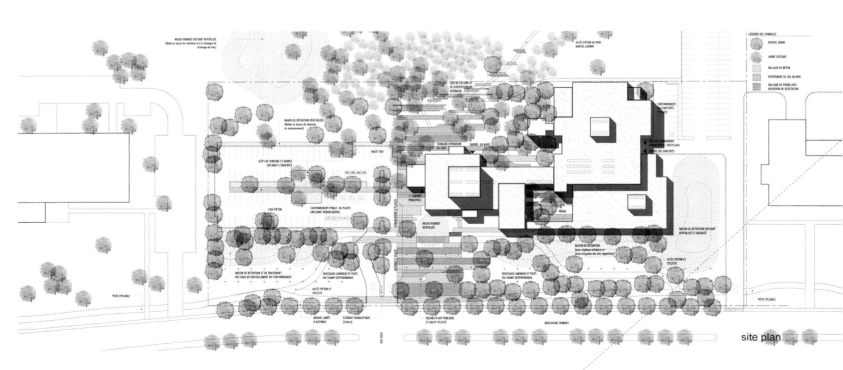

site plan

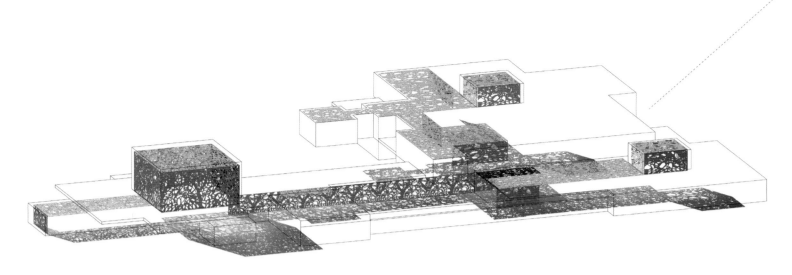

Instead of considering the new Saint-Laurent Library as "a gateway into Marcel-Laurin Park", the designers would rather imagine that it would become part of the park. In their opinion, the nature/culture dichotomy that leads to think that parks are green oasis's completely separated from the urban world by defined boundaries no longer corresponds to the aspirations of Montreal's citizens. The desire to make the city greener expands to streets, back alleys, backyards and rooftops and associates this willingness to sustainable design, quality of life and overall improvement of the city's vegetal coverage. Visiting the library can then become part of an immersive experience that contributes to this desire while offering a favourable environment for reading.

The buildings fragmented geometry allows it to blend into the existing forests, where, in particular, the cottonwoods have a life span of about twelve years. And to further contribute to its biodiversity, the disigners have proposed the planting of new varieties of trees. The library's perimeter would then be stretched to the main Boulevard so that the library could be set in the heart of the forest.

Forests provides green energy and create an air-and-noise filter. All the LED lights use solar energy. Rainwater retention surfaces are also designed to become part of the humid zones already present in Marcel-Laurin Park. Generous windows allow the user of the building to have constant visual contact with the surrounding forest. The library project offers an opportunity to create a green energy themed garden that would become a showcase of the best sustainable practices for people visiting the park recreationally or for those who walk by daily.

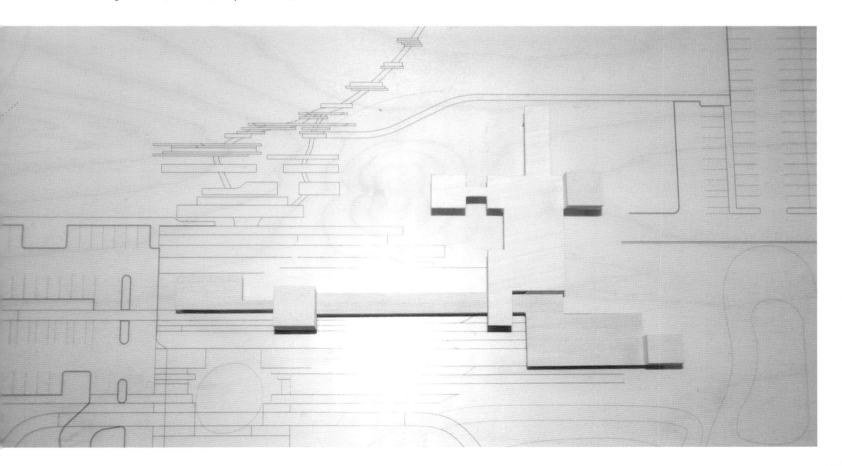

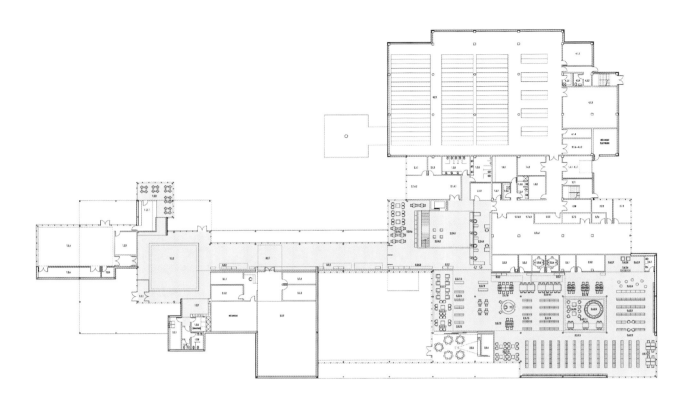

first floor plan

The project also includes museum storage for the city. This space is simple, rectangular and functional. Certain artefacts from the city's collections could be temporarily exposed the building's exhibition cabinets, in order to contribute making the library a lively and dynamic space.

The Periodical Room and the space used for selling books in the secondary hall also contributes making the library a public animated space, perfect for cultural exchanges while preserving a calm atmosphere associated to the delicate light, which is the key to the new library's identity.

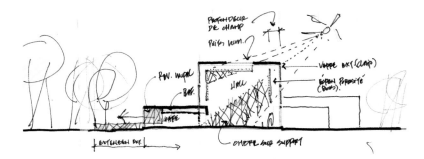

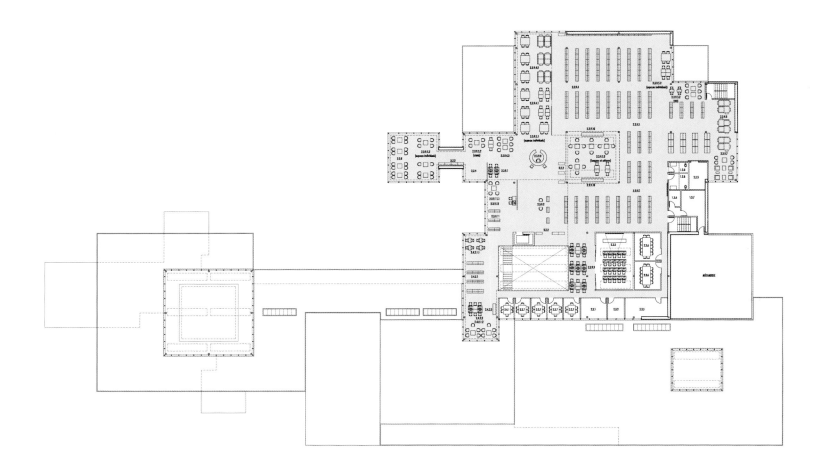

second floor plan

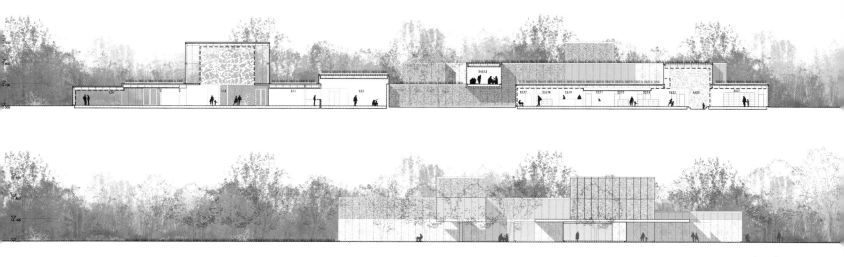

elevation

LIVRES D'IMAGES
Eab-Iwa

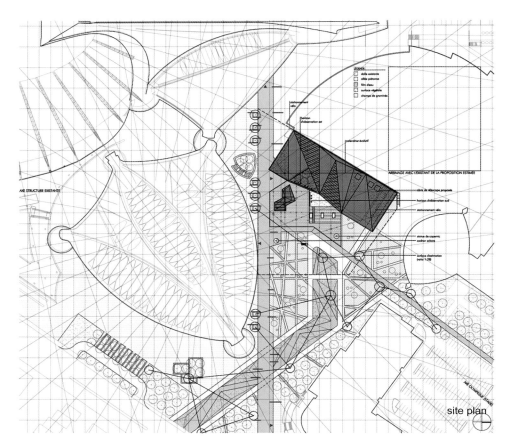

site plan

EXPOSING THE INTANGIBLE: GOING BEYOND WHITE BLINDNESS

The project takes its first inspiration in the very particular artificial site in which it is set. Through the complex network of existing structures, the planetarium blends into the white universe of the Olympic installations. In contrast to the opaque and matt concrete used for the Olympic stadium and for the cycling installations, the planetarium is translucent and milky.

With human activity, the interior will be invaded by colors and the many polished and reflective surfaces,

like opalescent glass, stainless steel, white perforated aluminium and frit glass, will contribute to amplify this effect. Once inside, articulated volumes and spaces will reveal the object of the museum: the Star theatres, covered in perforated brass panels.

Inspired by today's climate changes and melting arctic ice, the building resembles a tormented and cracked rectangular volume. Slowly sinking next to the Olympic stadium on one side, it seems to be in a precarious balance on the other.

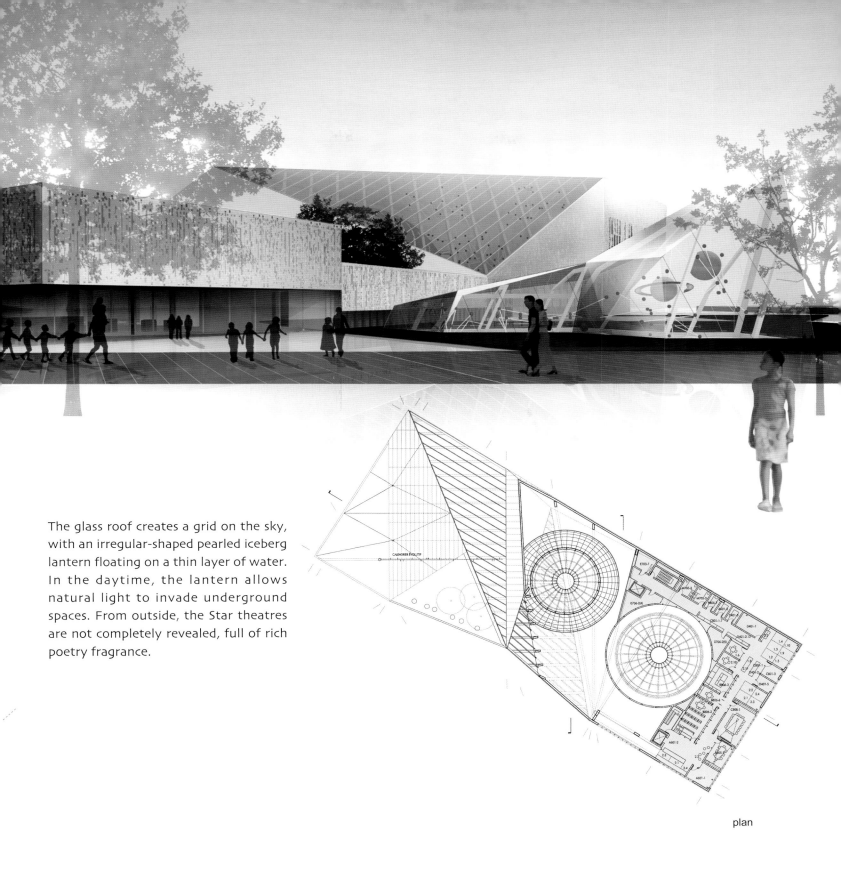

The glass roof creates a grid on the sky, with an irregular-shaped pearled iceberg lantern floating on a thin layer of water. In the daytime, the lantern allows natural light to invade underground spaces. From outside, the Star theatres are not completely revealed, full of rich poetry fragrance.

plan

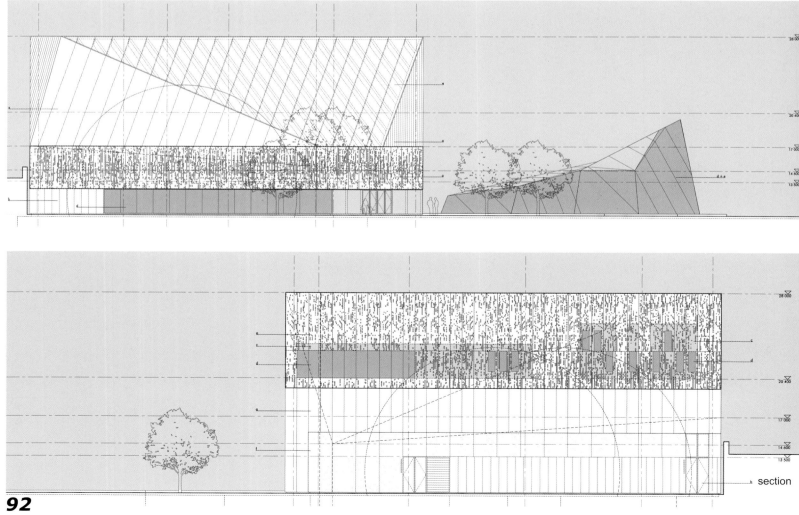

section

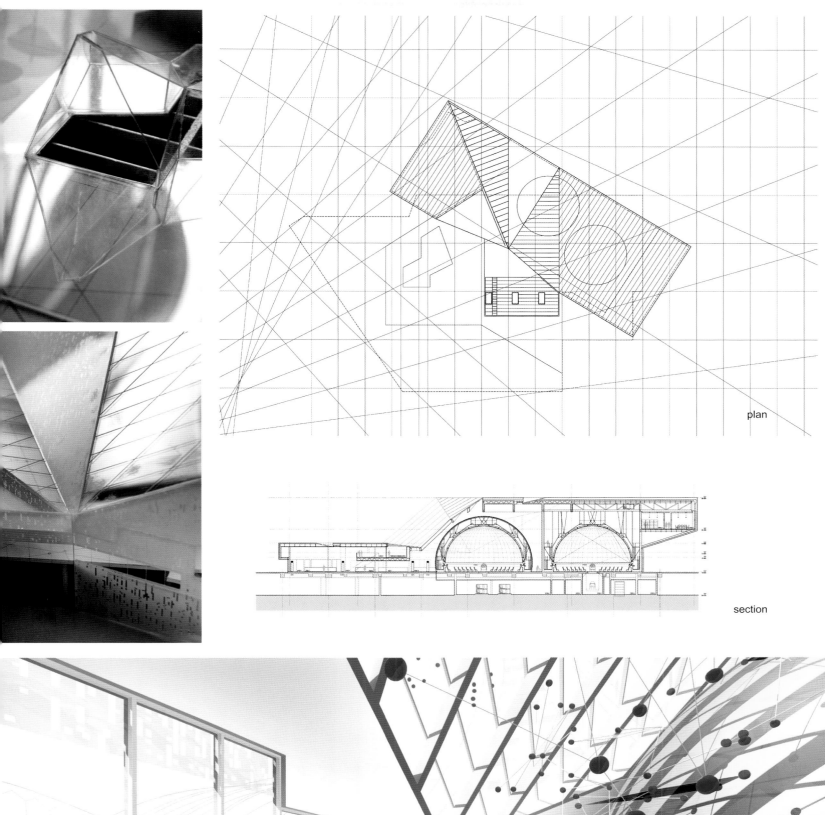

plan

section

Architects: Tétreault Parent Languedoc, Saia Barbarese Topouzanov Architects

UQAM CAMPUS

The original master plan for the UQAM Campus, prepared in 1991, invoked the image of a traditional campus, that of a central green space surrounded by buildings, according to the classic model of several universities. This layout enabled the complex both to fit into its environment and set itself apart from it, while providing the tranquility needed for pursuing studies and research.

The original idea of a green space was transformed into a continuum of yards and gardens enclosed inside buildings or interspersed between them. The green space also includes paths and a pedestrian walkway set up along the forgotten traces of what was once Kimberly Street and the extension of Evans Street. Nature has insinuated herself into these man-made structures. All these spaces come together, giving structure to the architecture and bathing

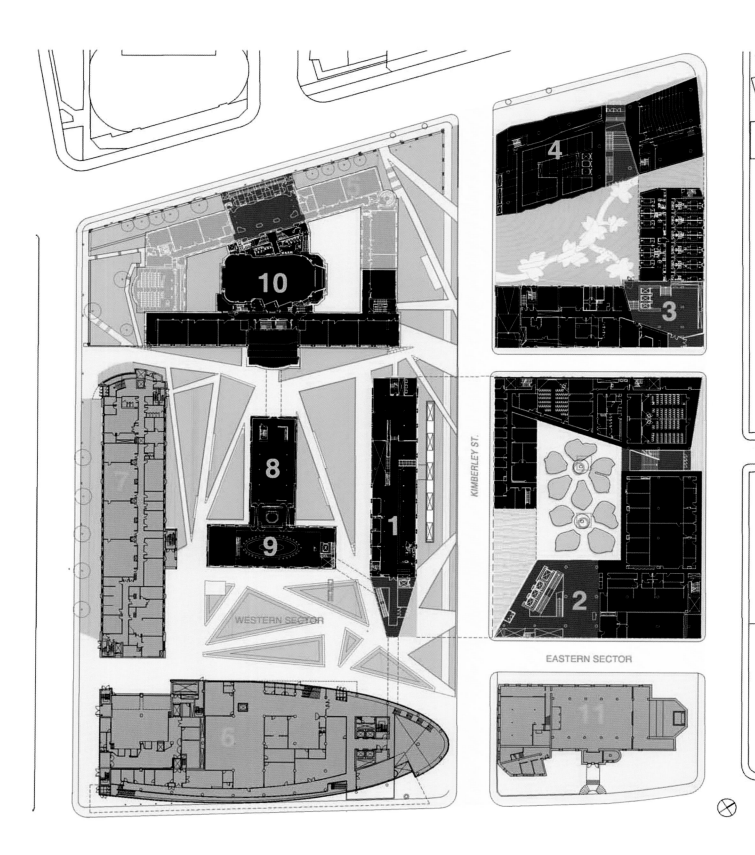

KIMBERLEY ST.

WESTERN SECTOR

EASTERN SECTOR

1. central library
2. biological science building
3. student residence
4. broadcasting building
5. sherbrooke building
6. president-kennedy building

7. biochemistry building
8. mediatech
9. student cafe
10. new auditorium
11. st-john the evangelist church

existing building
intervention
interior public spaces

plan

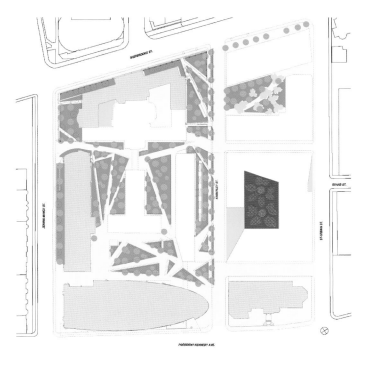

landscape plan

them in light. Their intertwined networks link street accesses to the entrances of the various pavilions. The spaces provide intimate settings, which are ideal for meetings, discussions, relaxation and reflection. The busy paths are lined with rows of trees, whose irregular patterns evoke the forest. In the gardens, giant flowers, some of them made of slate, pave the walkways between the buildings (student residences' garden), while other form petals around a tree assume the role of a giant pistil (Biological Sciences Pavilion yard). Indigenous species or plants of botanical interest have been selected for their ability to adapt to the urban climate. They introduce greenery within the city, in a neighborhood that is in desperate need of foliage.

In short, the traditional shape of campuses is evolving: the new configuration is one in which spaces overlap, and where spaces and erected structures are architectural equals.

Architect: WZMH Architects

Landscape Architect: Quinn Design Associates Interior Designer: Cannon Design

Structural Engineer: Halsall Associates Limited

Location: Oshawa, Ontario, Canada

Area: 41,957 m²

Photographer: Shai Gil

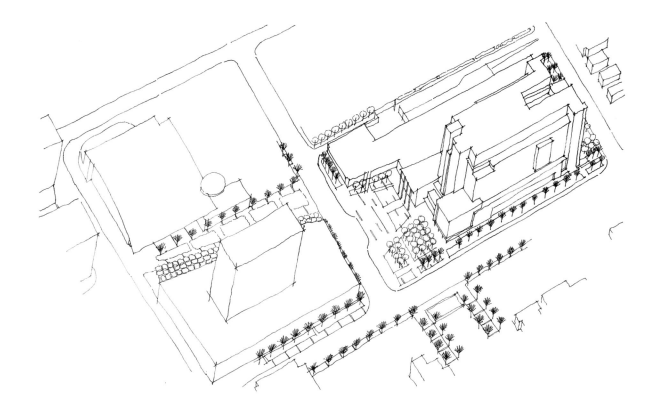

DURHAM CONSOLIDATED COURTHOUSE

With its richly patterned cladding of spandrel, clear glass massing, Durham Consolidated Courthouse, completed in January 2010, makes a significant contribution to the emerging urban framework of downtown Oshawa. Its bold, modern vocabulary emphasizes transparency and openness both for users and passersby.

A large outdoor public space, Courthouse square, is the forecourt to the building entrance. The scale of the main entrance pavilion on the square establishes a sense of dignity, appropriate for the front door of a courthouse.

Providing badly-needed space for the province´s judicial system, this six-storey, 40,000 m² structure houses 33 courtrooms, associated support space and prisoner-holding facilities.

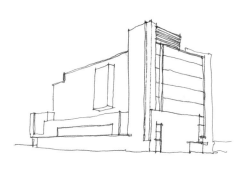

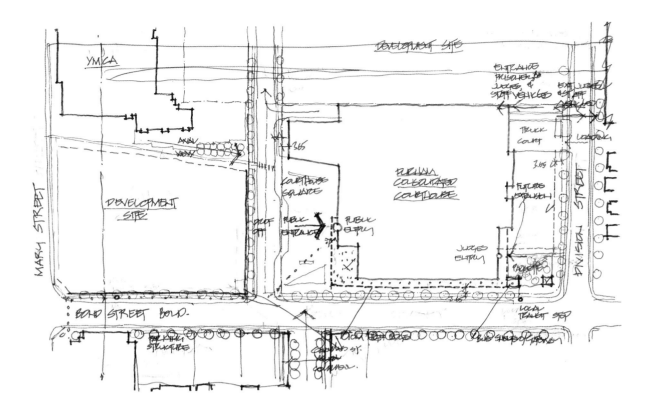

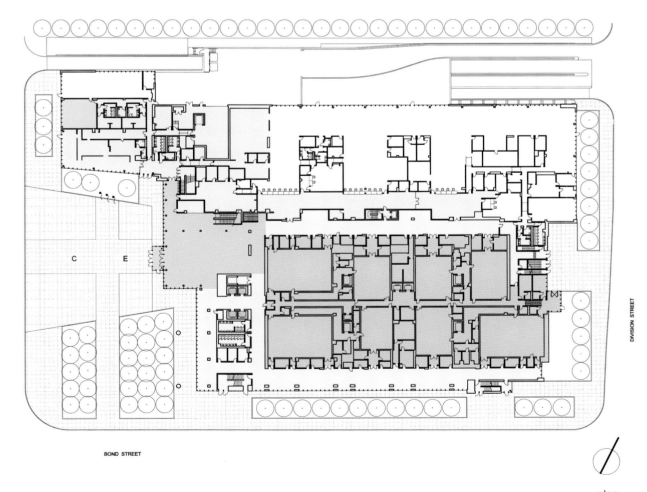

plan

109

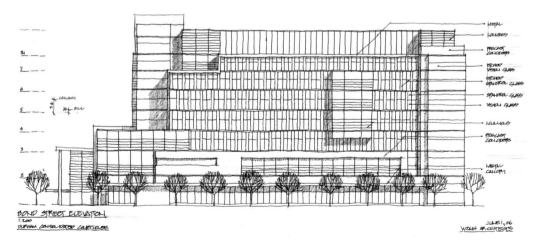

BOND STREET ELEVATION
1:200
DURHAM CONSOLIDATED COURTHOUSE

JUNE 1, 06
WZMH ARCHITECTS

COURTHOUSE STREET ELEVATION
1:200
DURHAM CONSOLIDATED COURTHOUSE

elevation

The courthouse represents a physical embodiment of our justice system interpreted in a modernist language. Solid building elements serve to express the stability and permanence of the courts. Welcoming to the public, the courthouse elevations are highly transparent, using clear glass with a rich mosaic of white ceramic frit glass panels. The scale of the main entrance pavilion creates a formality and sense of dignity, appropriate for the front door of a courthouse.

On the west, the main building core is raised to create a visual terminus, looking east from the proposed linear park. At the southeast corner of the site, a column of glass that is illuminated at night creates a strong gateway to downtown Oshawa.

The project exhibits a new typology for a typical courtroom floor that has a "back to back" arrangement of courtrooms that results in short walking distances for judges and staff. The availability of daylight and views to the outside in the courtroom waiting areas will reduce stress for the participants in court proceedings.

elevation

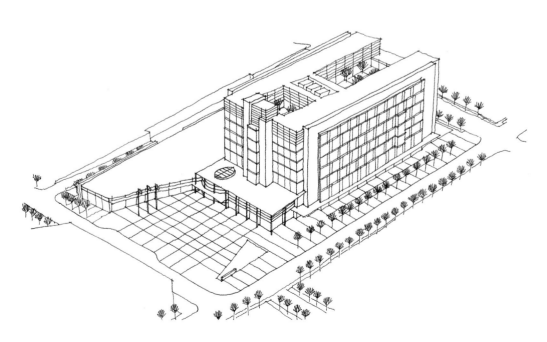

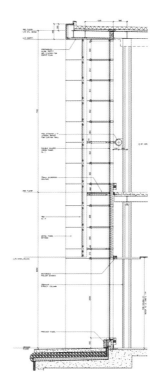

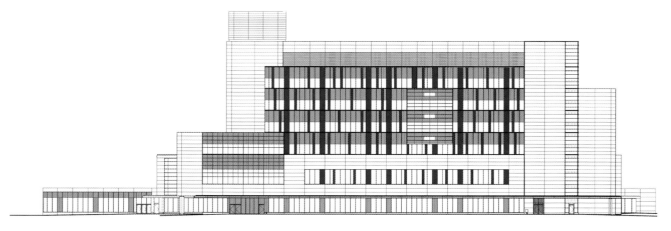

south elevation

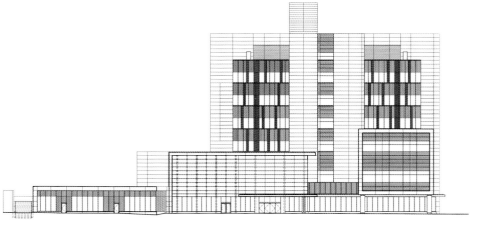

west elevation

113

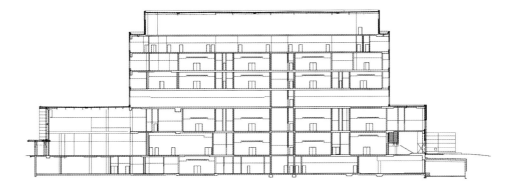

east-west section

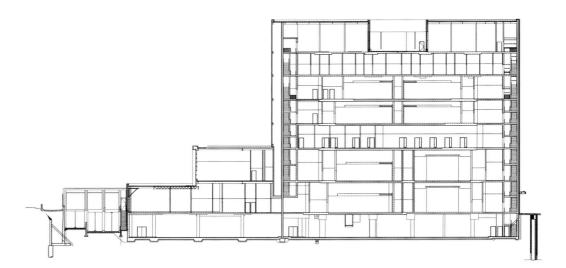

north-south section

Architect: Kleinfeldt Mychajlowycz Architects Inc.

Location: Brampton, Ontario, Canda

Area: 20,438 m²

Photographer: A-Frame Studio

ROY MCMURTRY YOUTH CENTRE

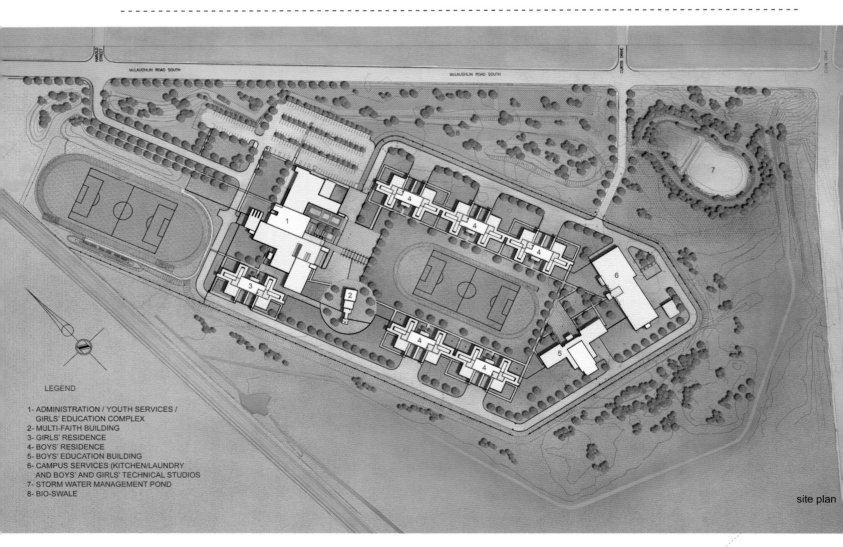

LEGEND

1- ADMINISTRATION / YOUTH SERVICES /
   GIRLS' EDUCATION COMPLEX
2- MULTI-FAITH BUILDING
3- GIRLS' RESIDENCE
4- BOYS' RESIDENCE
5- BOYS' EDUCATION BUILDING
6- CAMPUS SERVICES (KITCHEN/LAUNDRY
   AND BOYS' AND GIRLS' TECHNICAL STUDIOS
7- STORM WATER MANAGEMENT POND
8- BIO-SWALE

site plan

The decision made in 2004 by the Provincial Government of Ontario to introduce a new Ministry of Child and Youth Services, as distinct from the adult facilities, has allowed a re-evaluation of the programs and physical expression of them in consideration of youth offenders.

The site is an existing 400,000 m2 institutional site which was initially surrounded by agricultural fields. The site is cleared of an existing women's prison, with the exception of two buildings, which were maintained and renovated as part of the Youth Centre. Eight new buildings have been added to the site to provide services to 192 youth offenders, 32 girls and boys, aged 12 years to 17 years old. Over 300 staff members, volunteers and family members and visitors are included in the immediate community of the centre.

The secured area of the site is a Campus Morphology, reinforcing the education ideals of the centre. A garden is located in the centre. Contiguous buildings, infill board-formed concrete, masonry panels and Corten steel panels define the garden wall. The Campus is surrounded by a public park, offering a naturalized landscape including a bio-swale, pond, existing mature trees, hundreds of new trees and a new streetscape. Campus Morphology is critical to the success of this Youth Centre, both in promoting a healthy public understanding of the ideals of the institution and the residents understanding of their place and obligations in the society.

Architect: Consortium KPMB FSA

Location: Montreal, Quebec, Canada

JOHN MOLSON SCHOOL OF BUSINESS

After opening its doors officially for the first time on September 22, John Molson Business School unveiled its new facilities to students and public alike in the "Quartier Concordia" area of Downtown Montreal. The firms of Kuwabara Payne McKenna Blumberg Architects and Fichten Soiferman Associates formed a consortium, KPMB / FSA, for this leading green project. This project boasting world class environmental technology, as well as state-of-the-art facilities for faculty and students is part of a three-phase project including the Guy Metro Building and the Engineering-Computer Science and Visual Arts Integrated Complex. All the three are inter-linked underground and connected to the STM Metro system.

Within its two sub-basement levels and 15 levels above ground, there are 45 state-of-the-art classrooms, a 300-seat auditorium, two 150-seat amphitheaters, four 120-seat amphitheaters, 22 conference rooms, and numerous other office spaces and services housed within the complex.

This exemplary building includes many features that have contributed to its candidacy for a LEED designation, which is currently under review. Many components ranging from the use of durable materials like granite, metal, glass and ceramic, and the use of high performance thermal glass on its exterior address this "green" sensibility in very practical ways. In addition, KPMB / FSA have integrated a green roof on the 4th floor terrace. What's more, the architects have also incorporated solar panels that were developed at Concordia, on the top of one of the facades of the large structure. This solar wall produces enough energy to significantly reduce the energy consumption of the building; and is equivalent to heating seven Canadian homes throughout the year.

MCGILL UNIVERSITY LIFE SCIENCES COMPLEX

The primary function of the McGill University Life Sciences Complex is research in cancer and biomedicine. This includes five key components: chemical biology, complex traits, developmental biology, cell information systems and cancer research. The Complex integrates the new facilities, the Francesco Bellini Life Sciences Building and the Cancer Research Building, as well as the existing McIntyre Medical Sciences and Stewart Biological Sciences buildings.

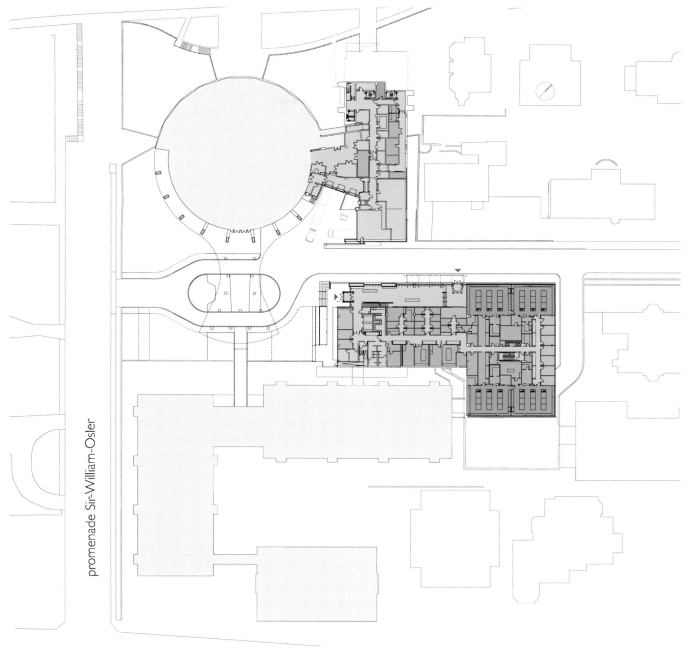

promenade Sir-William-Osler

Linking elements and informal social spaces tie the new facility to both adjacent buildings. At the upper levels, this allows for research inter-connectivity. At the lower, more public levels, these spaces encourage casual interaction between users during breaks. The four-storey interior atrium space doubles as a pedestrian passage, leading to vertical circulation into the complex and enhancing social and academic campus life.

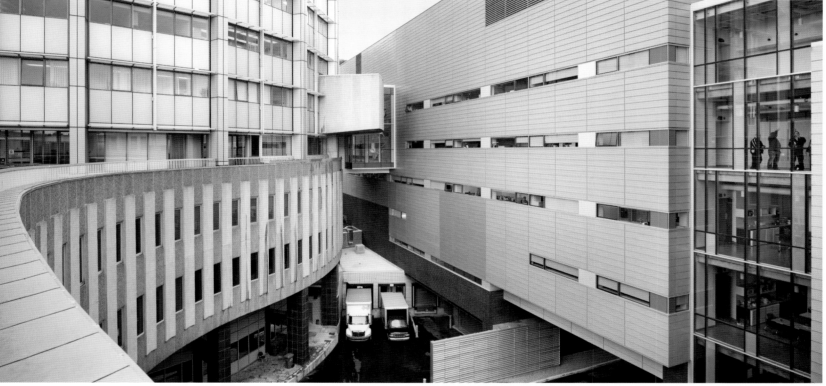

The Life Sciences Complex is sited adjacent to one of the most cherished green spaces in Montreal – the upper slopes of Mount Royal. The sensitive context, coupled with the University's sustainable building mandate and the architects' commitment to reducing the ecological impact of architecture, helped to establish the design team's goal of constructing an unobtrusive energy efficient building. The new Bellini and Cancer pavilions are designed to achieve LEED Gold certification with the Canadian Green Building Council.

An integrated design approach, including value management sessions, have been utilized to ensure architectural integration of sustainable design features and to fully understand the impact each decision would have on operating and maintenance costs during the life of the building. Each energy conservation measure was considered individually, based on a 10-year payback benchmark. Overall, the total building will use 53kWh/m2 annually, 36% more efficient than the Canadian National Model Energy Code reference building, deserving to be the exemplary model of the energy-efficient architecture.

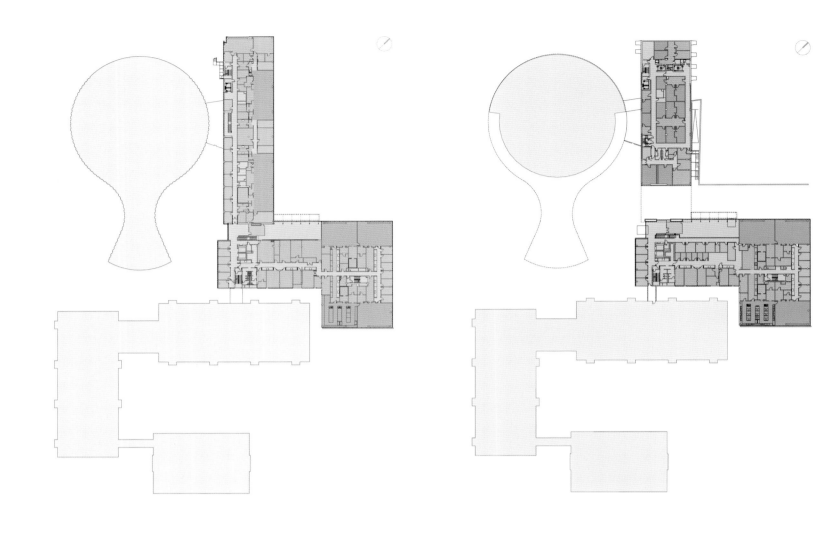

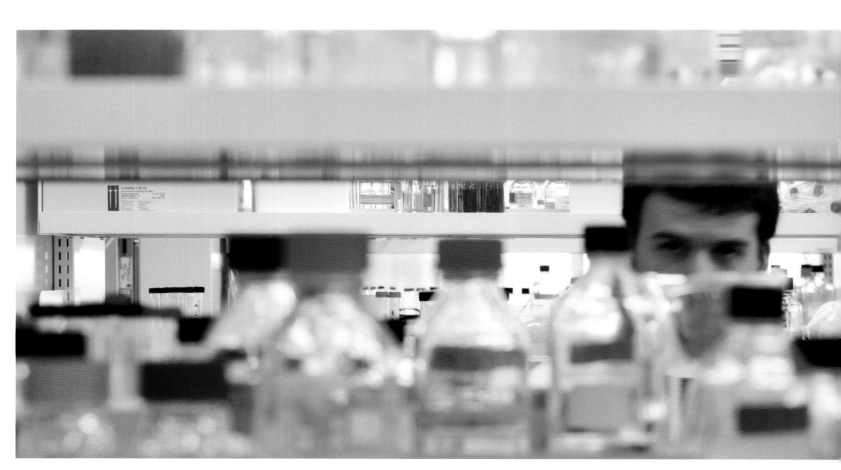

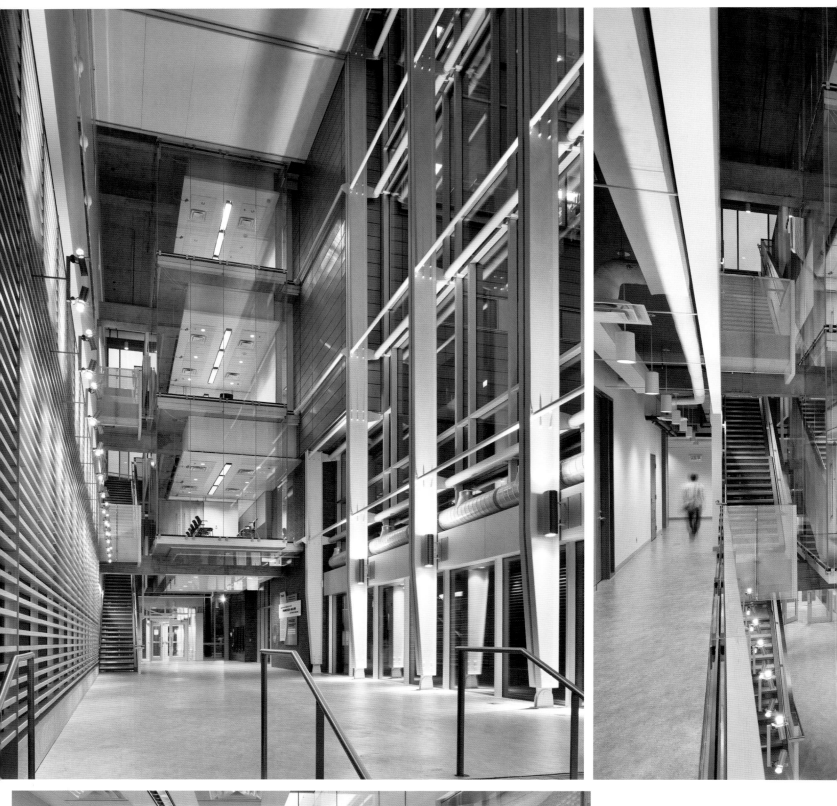

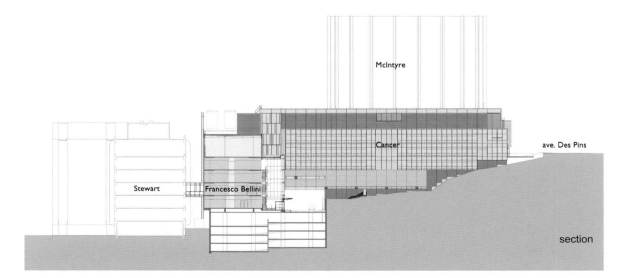

McIntyre

Cancer

ave. Des Pins

Stewart

Francesco Bellini

section

Architects: Fournier, Gersovitz, Moss, Drolet et Associates Architects

D'ÉTUDES NORDIQUES COMMUNITY SCIENCE CENTRE

The centre is devoted to scientific research and exchange of traditional knowledge.

One of the most significant part of the centre is that a hall was designed specifically to host school groups of all levels for teaching activities and popularization of science; the hall will also display a permanent exhibition describing the territory's cultural and scientific history.

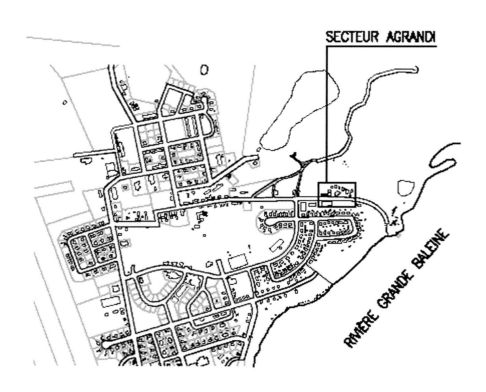

SECTEUR AGRANDI

RIVIÈRE GRANDE BALEINE

Sustainable development and conservation of nature are not new practices, especially in a hostile northern environment devoid of resources and fragile. Transportation of materials is difficult, the construction season is short, and climatic constraints impose specific logistical solutions. Well versed in construction in northern regions, FGMDA designed an efficient building that respects the environment and reduces energy consumption thanks to passive solar heating, abundant south-facing fenestration, floors used as thermal mass,

and integration of photovoltaic cells.

An exterior envelope presenting high levels of thermal resistance and airtightness is essential when temperatures drop below -40°C. Wood is used for both the frame and the exterior envelope (red cedar cladding, pine substructure, and yellow birch panelling). In addition, the integration of a double vestibule at each entrance reduces air exchanges and helps to conserve energy.

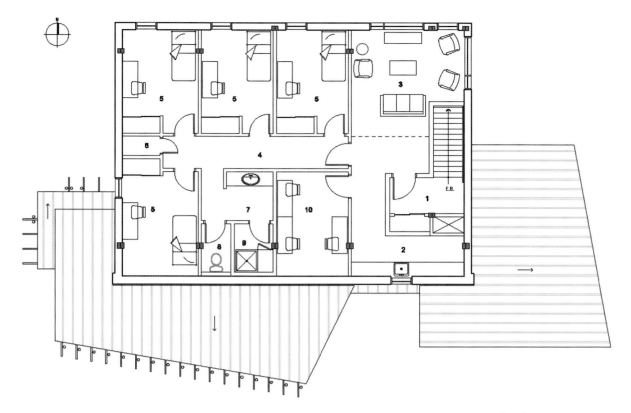

first floor plan

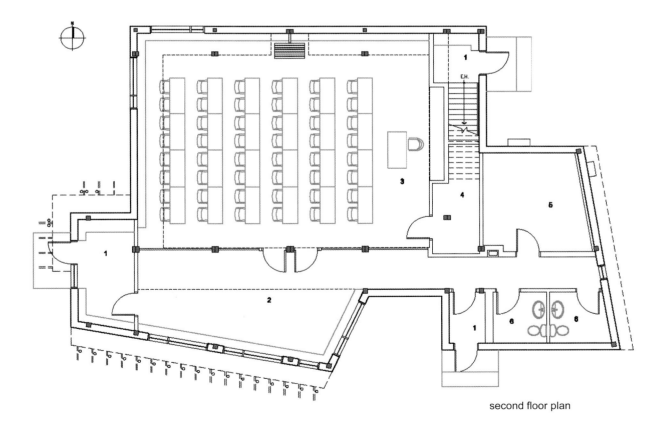

second floor plan

141

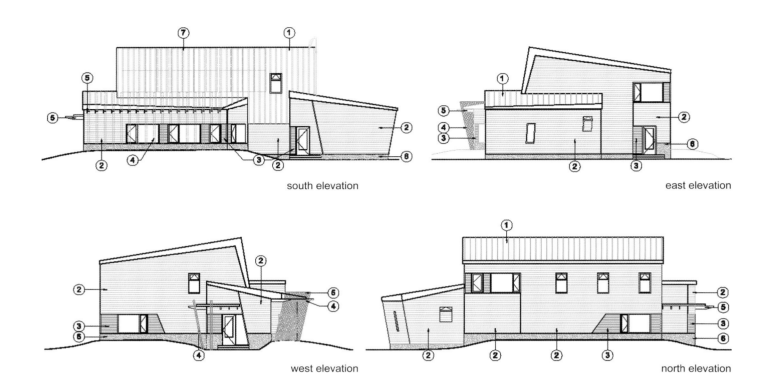

south elevation

east elevation

west elevation

north elevation

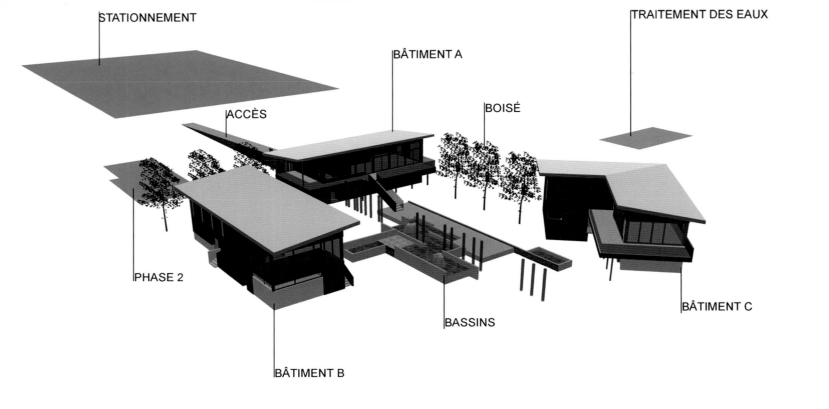

STATIONNEMENT

TRAITEMENT DES EAUX

BÂTIMENT A

ACCÈS

BOISÉ

PHASE 2

BASSINS

BÂTIMENT C

BÂTIMENT B

Office lofts

Hanging
wood screens

Access
bridges

Water
features

Geothermal
well field

COMMERCE

Green roof

South grove

Parkade

Public plaza

LUXURY, SERENITY AND INNOVATION: LE GERMAIN CALGARY HOTEL

The Le Germain Calgary Hotel boasts an exceptional and excellent location in the heart of downtown. Connected to the city's network of elevated pedestrian walkways, the hotel, unlike other Germain hotels, actually opens directly on to 9th Avenue. The lobby features a two-story glass wall facing the main commercial street, thus creating a unique vibrancy between the street and the hotel space.

The materials and interior design were selected to combine ease and comfort. "Our goal was to create a welcoming environment with a flash of innovation," the designer explains. The hotel's exterior cladding of Prodema wood-laminate panels prefigures the warmth of the interiors. Beyond the impressive fenestration of the façade, the main entrance is a vibrant, active space, perfectly bringing the beautiful outside world into the hotel.

Between the lobby and front desk area, a wall of recycled felt, in shades of grey and black resembling shale, adds both texture and acoustic properties. The whole hotel as if is sleeping in a cradle, sweetly and happily.

In addition, 90 wells are drilled to supply the hotel with enough geothermal energy to heat the water and some radiant floors. All rooms are equipped with the technological necessities of the modern travelers (e.g., Internet access, flat-screen television), facilitating guests to keep in touch with the outside world.

The hotel embodies a splendid experience of luxury, serenity and innovation.

1. lobby
2. lounge
3. restaurant
4. administration

site plan

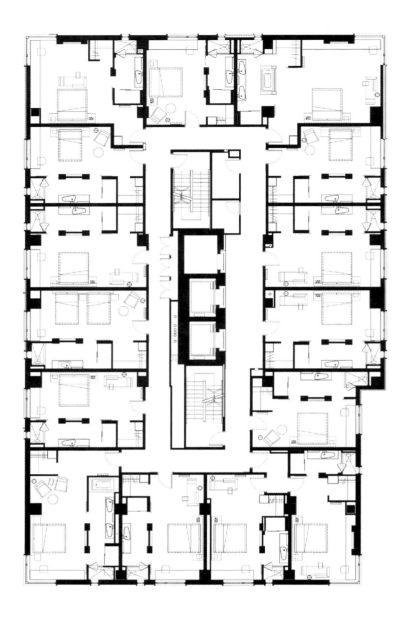

floor plan

Architect: Chevalier Morales Architects

Engineers: Les Consultants Gemec, Génivar

Project Managers: Sergio Morales, Stephan Chevalier

Project Team: Sergio Morales, Stephan Chevalier, Karine Dieujuste, Christine Giguère, Samantha Hayes, Neil Melendez

Location: Montreal, Quebec, Canada

Area: 1,000 m²

Photographer: Marc Cramer

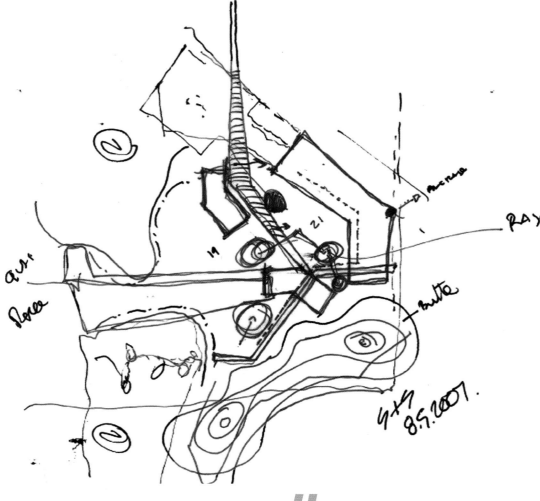

STRÖM SPA NORDIQUE

Exterior spas seem to be taking a more important place in people's life compared to traditional theme parks.

Ström Spa Nordique provides this new type of playground for the body and mind offers a sensitive contemporary design. Three separate buildings are placed delicately on the manmade topography and look out onto the Lac des Battures. The buildings are occupied by saunas, massage and relaxation rooms, Turkish baths and other spaces necessary to make a functional spa. Covered in clay grey brick and white wood, the buildings exude calm and serenity. Brass elements like strange sculptures, gargoyles and interior furniture are making reference to all piping, hid underground or in mechanical rooms, responsible for the magical experience that offers the spa.

At night, the blend of neon lights, LED lighting and flames of torches illuminates the surreal décor, lightly and brightly.

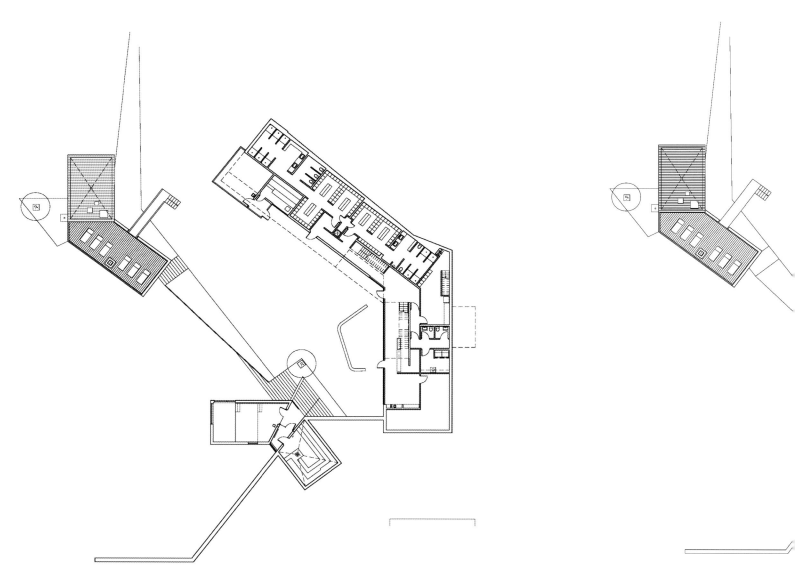

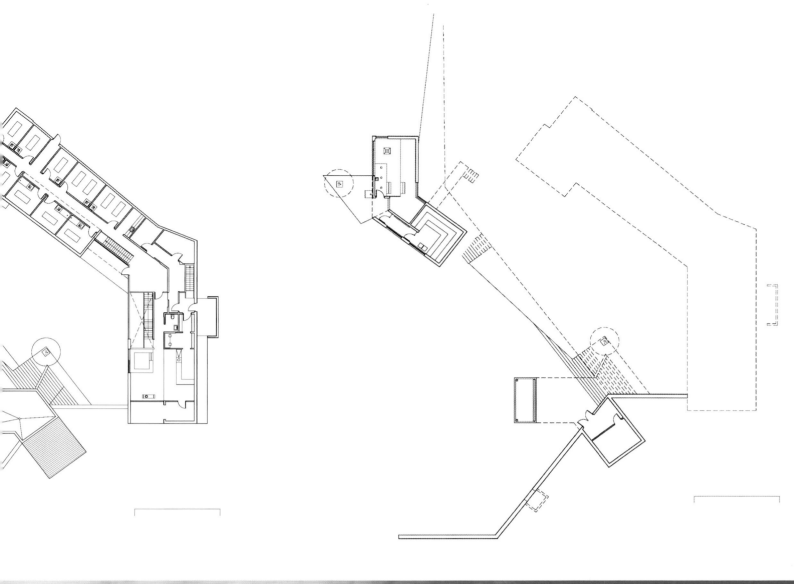

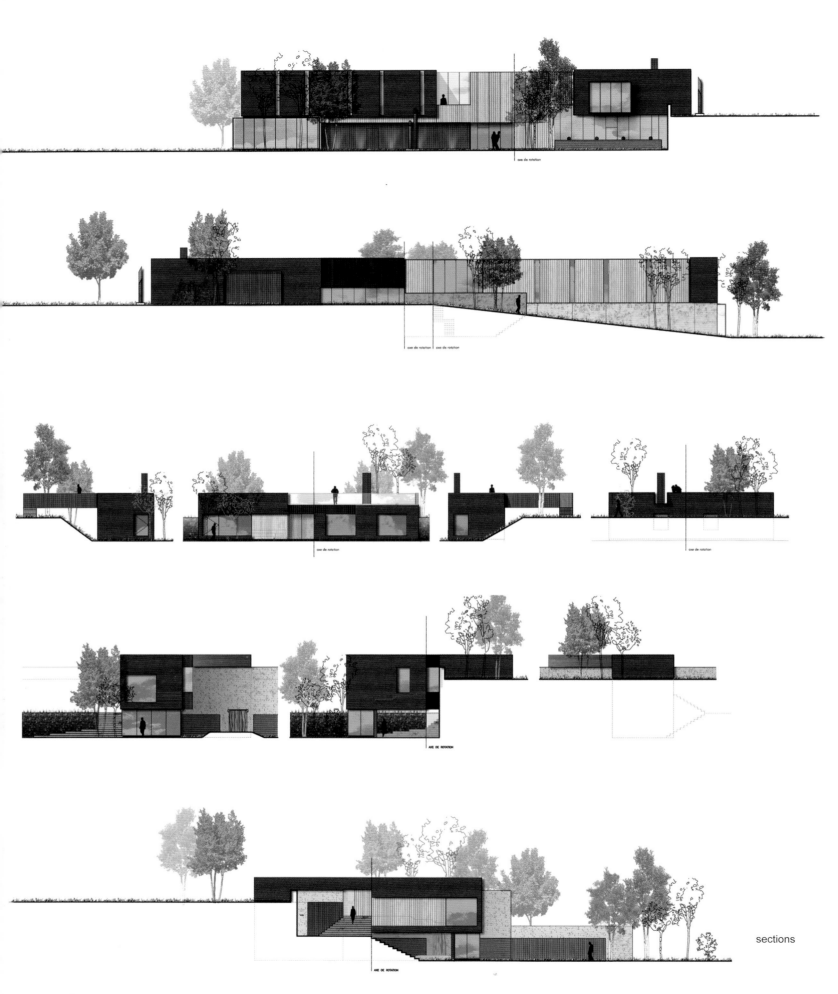

sections

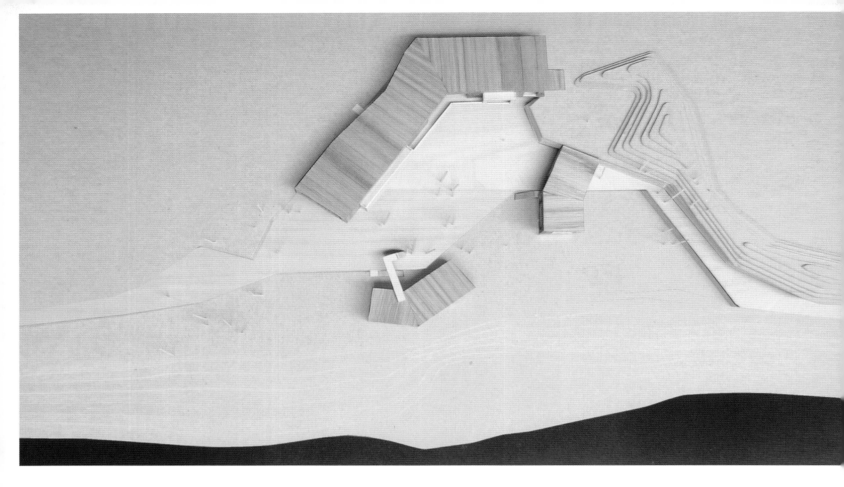

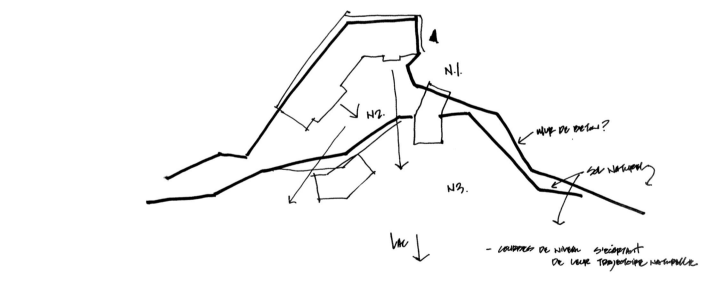

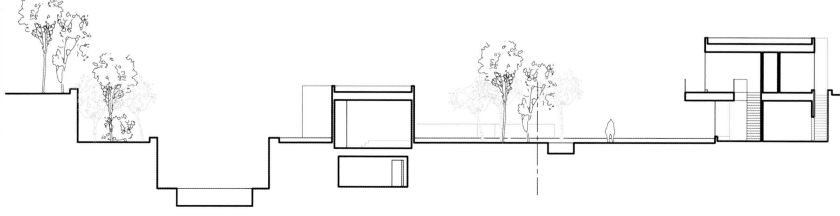

Architect: Cibinel Architects Ltd.

Landscape Architects: Hilderman Thomas, Frank Cram Landscape Architecture & Planning

Engineers: Crosier Kilgour & Partners Ltd, Epp Siepman Engineering Inc, Nova 3 Engineering Ltd, Williams Engineering Inc, M. Block & Associates Ltd.

Location: 12 – 19th Street North, Brandon, Manitoba, Canada

Area: about 2,000 m²

Photographer: Mike Karakas

BRANDON NO.1 FIREHALL

The dynamic new 2,800 m² Brandon Fire and Emergency Services Building validates the idea that a primarily utilitarian program, which often times results in a prefabricated solution, can become a sophisticated architectural project that contributes to its surrounding community and landscape while still fulfilling its demanding functional requirements and modest budget.

The facility is divided into two formal components, a fire hall wing and an administrative wing. The separation allows daylight to penetrate the buildings on all sides, and a single-loaded corridor animates the façade with human movement and activity. A minimally detailed, non-programmed transparent volume situated between the two wings acts as a dramatic entry into both sections of the facility, mediating the two programs with a thin hovering glulam bridge.

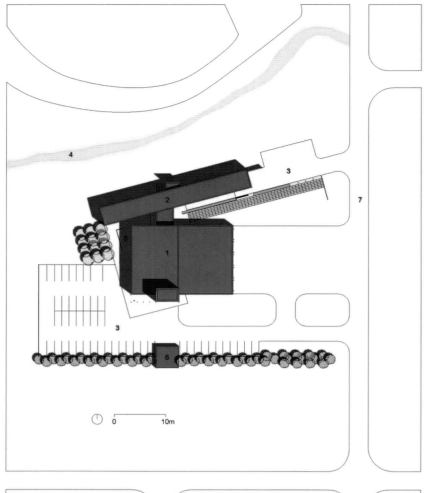

1. fire hall
2. administrative wing
3. parking
4. creek

5. outdoor space
6. cold storage
7. 19th street

site plan

The public entry engages and welcomes the community with a generous landscaped public "plaza" enclosed by the museum to the north, and the apparatus floor to the south. The museum features a "Bickle", an 80-year-old fire truck situated as if it is ready to take off to the next call, while the apparatus floor houses the current emergency fleet. Extensive glazing surrounding the plaza highlights the rich history of the fire department in the city, and allows visitors a glance into a state of the art facility.

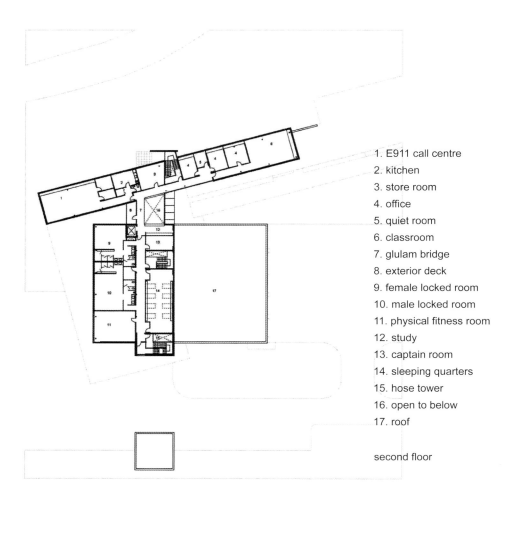

1. E911 call centre
2. kitchen
3. store room
4. office
5. quiet room
6. classroom
7. glulam bridge
8. exterior deck
9. female locked room
10. male locked room
11. physical fitness room
12. study
13. captain room
14. sleeping quarters
15. hose tower
16. open to below
17. roof

second floor

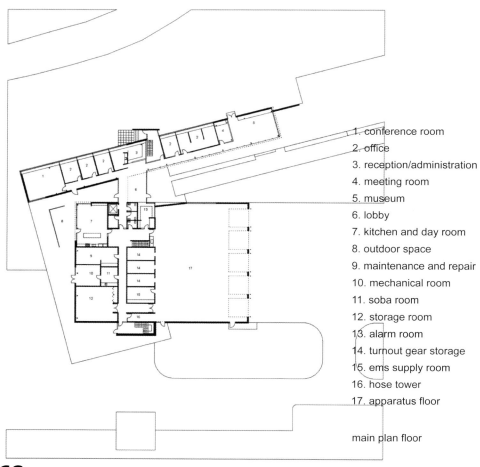

1. conference room
2. office
3. reception/administration
4. meeting room
5. museum
6. lobby
7. kitchen and day room
8. outdoor space
9. maintenance and repair
10. mechanical room
11. soba room
12. storage room
13. alarm room
14. turnout gear storage
15. ems supply room
16. hose tower
17. apparatus floor

main plan floor

A dramatic hose tower stands proud in the landscape and acts as an urban marker for people entering the city along the neighboring street. Impervious dark brick cladding descends the tower and wraps around the building's horizontal walking surfaces, allowing for a natural runoff of water to be reabsorbed by the site's indigenous grasses.

The solution integrates functionality seamlessly into the aesthetics, giving appropriate expression to the demands of the facility while creating unique and effective civic presence in the community.

LES LOFTS
REDPATH

Les Lofts Redpath is located on the banks of the Lachine canal in Montreal. On a larger scale, the project constitutes a residential block composed of commercial spaces on the main floor. Though encountered by amid technical challenges, the developer still wanted to pursue the construction of residential lofts within these industrial brushlands. The current residents of the complex appreciate its specific industrial character and the exceptional attractions of the sector: the banks of the canal that have re-opened to nautical activities, amazing views of the mountain and downtown, a linear park, a bike path, etc.

The commercial spaces have distinct entrances that give directly onto the courtyard. The presence of commercial spaces also encourages contact with the canal's public spaces.

The courtyard constitutes a transition gateway as much for the residents as for the public. Its simple and elegant layout reinforces the architectural sobriety of the whole.

The courtyard is mainly composed of a grass garden, vines and shrubs, punctuated by willows suggesting the presence of water.

The group of buildings serves as a complex of business, industrialization and residence. It complies with the sustainable principle, enhances work efficiency, and provides convenience to its residents and business circulation, embodying a significant model for the city architecture.

The project has been awarded the Finalist for the Awards of Excellence 2007 of the Ordre des Architects du Quebec, and represents a cultural interest recognized by Park Council of Canada and the City of Montreal.

MANITOBA HYDRO PLACE

Manitoba Hydro Place This is a world-class office tower which is a model for the next generation of extreme climate responsive architecture. Designed by the integrated design consortium of Kuwabara Payne McKenna Blumberg Architects (Toronto), Smith Carter Architects (Winnipeg), Transsolar Klima Engineering (Stuttgart), the tower has already gained attention with the prestigious "Best Tall Building in North America" award that is granted by the CTBUH (Council for Tall Buildings), the world's leading body dedicated to the field of tall buildings and urban habitat. Already generating international interest, the project has appeared in the Princeton University Press, the Architectural Press, and various other journals in Europe and Asia.

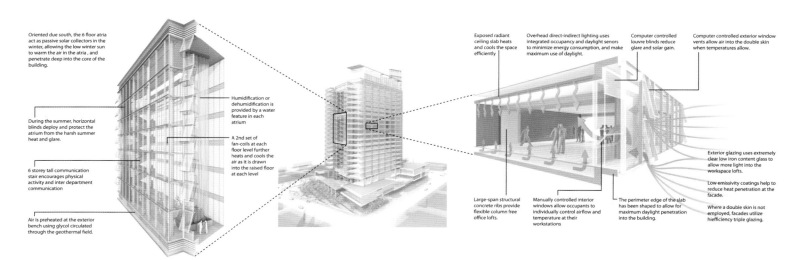

Oriented due south, the 6 floor atria act as passive solar collectors in the winter, allowing the low winter sun to warm the air in the atria , and penetrate deep into the core of the building.

During the summer, horizontal blinds deploy and protect the atrium from the harsh summer heat and glare.

6 storey tall communication stair encourages physical activity and inter department communication

Air is preheated at the exterior bench using glycol circulated through the geothermal field.

Humidification or dehumidification is provided by a water feature in each atrium

A 2nd set of fan-coils at each floor level further heats and cools the air as it is drawn into the raised floor at each level

Exposed radiant ceiling slab heats and cools the space efficiently

Overhead direct-indirect lighting uses integrated occupancy and daylight senors to minimize energy consumption, and make maximum use of daylight.

Computer controlled louvre blinds reduce glare and solar gain.

Computer controlled exterior window vents allow air into the double skin when temperatures allow.

Large-span structural concrete ribs provide flexible column free office lofts.

Manually controlled interior windows allow occupants to individually control airflow and temperature at their workstations

The perimeter edge of the slab has been shaped to allow for maximum daylight penetration into the building.

Exterior glazing uses extremely clear low iron content glass to allow more light into the workspace lofts.

Low emissivity coatings help to reduce heat penetration at the facade.

Where a double skin is not employed, facades utilize hiefficiency triple glazing.

Winnipeg, located in the geographic centre of North America is one of the coldest large cities in the world. From the start, in 2003 the client, Manitoba Hydro, established ambitious goals and mandated the project be conducted within a formal Integrated Design Process (IDP). It was to be designed to optimize passive free energy and 100% fresh air year round in an extreme climate that fluctuates from -35°c to 34°c and without compromise the comfort of 2,000 employees. The design integrates tested environmental concepts in conjunction with advance technologies to achieve a "living building" that dynamically optimizes its local climate.

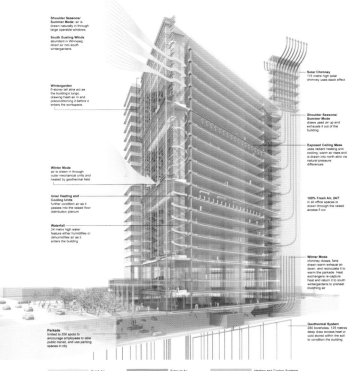

At the same time, it was to play a major role in the revitalization of the downtown, demonstrate architectural excellence, and most importantly demonstrate the client's recognition that its employees are its greatest asset by delivering a highly supportive, healthy workplace environment.

Office lofts

Hanging
wood screens

Access
bridges

Water
features

Green roof

South grove

Geothermal
well field

Parkade

Public plaza

183

Architects: Fournier, Gersovitz, Moss, Drolet et Associates Architects

Location: Hemmingford, Quebec, Canada

Area: 2,400 m²

CIDRERIE LA FACE CACHÉE DE LA POMME

Cidrerie la Face Cachée de la Pomme is a complex of argricultural production, family residence and travel.

In order to perfectly achieve these three functions, the project has three phases: architecture, landscape architecture and interior design.The architects respect the Scottish-inspired vernacular architecture, merging it with a resolutely modern, contemporary architectural language. Inspired by farms in southern Italy, the architects designed the residences and farm facilities to create a unity that is both aesthetic and functional. The yard can be a dock for unloading merchandise or be transformed into a tasting area for visitors. The grouping blends harmoniously into the landscape, enabling it to be a paradise for relaxing.

Sustainable development is part of the framework of the project, integral to both the facilities and the production processes. Particular attention was paid to the lighting; natural light was emphasized,which is particularly important for architectures under the cold climate. Therefore, Cidrerie la Face Cachée de la Pomme is located to the orientation which is towards plenty of natural light.

Architects: Brière, Gilbert + Associés Architectes

Location: Québec, Canada

REFURBISHMENT AND EXTENSION OF THE CRÉVHSL HEADQUARTERS

The project is defined in two parts:

The refurbishment of the existing building which accommodates several offices and the main reception and A contemporary extension to the rear, where the new

board room and the employee's cafeteria is located.

The refurbishment included mainly interior renovation and restoring to the original states the existing exterior doors and windows, and repairing the masonry and the roof.

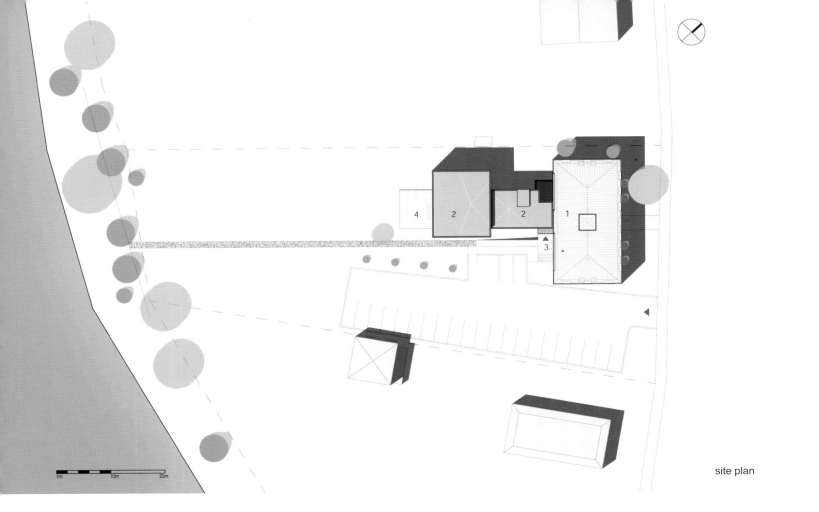

site plan

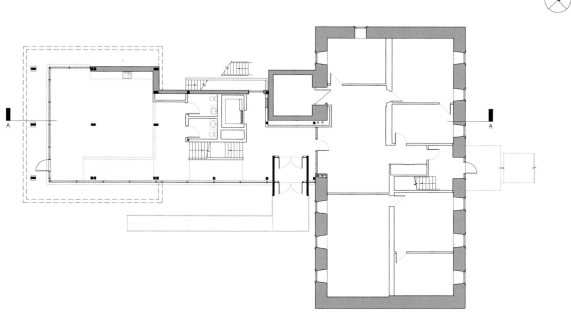

first floor plan

Three conceptual gestures helped to achieve these goals successfully:

First, the off-axis footprint, from the existing building of the extension, allows visual openings towards the St Lawrence river from both the new and existing building; Secondly, the "suspended" wooden volume, which wraps the new board room, provides an adequate response to the massive stone volume of the existing building; Thirdly, the integration of two atriums creates open spaces to accentuate the suspended wooden volume from the inside and opens views towards the river and site from the new and existing building.

The project includes sustainable development measures. The use of eastern Quebec cedar and wood for the exterior siding aims to enhance this natural resource of Québec. In addition, the project uses geothermal energy for heating, air conditioning, linked to heat recovery.

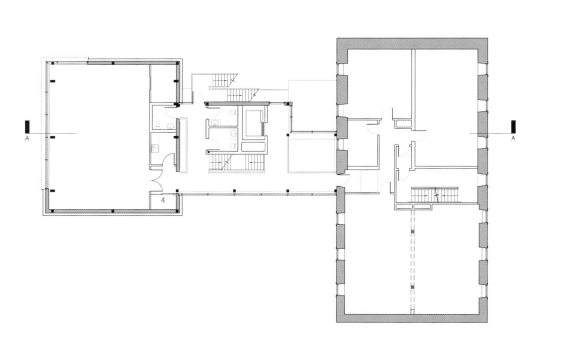

second floor plan

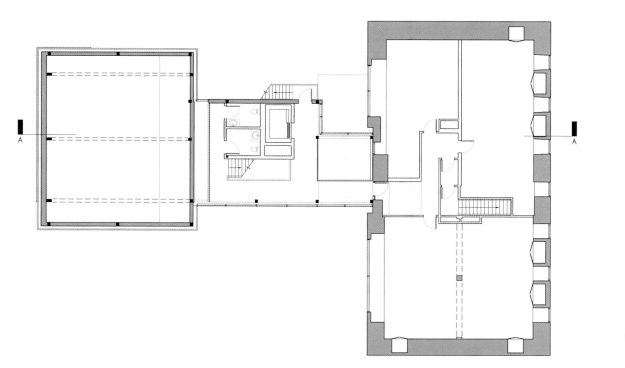

third floor plan

elevation

elevation

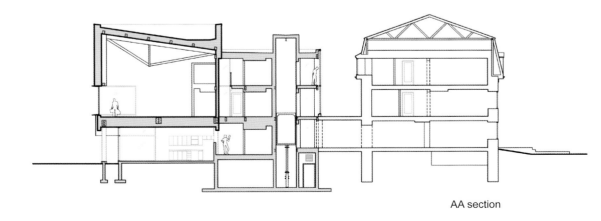

AA section

197

Architects: Blouin Tardif Architecture-Environnement

Location: Charltvoix, Quebec, Canada

Photographer: Stéphane Groleau

STATION BLÜ

This resort complex situated on the outskirts of the Charlevoix region includes a restaurant, steam bath, sauna, massage areas, hot and cold pools, and many relaxation spaces. These functions are shared among three pavilions articulated around a landscaped area bordering the river.

To unify the project grouping, the buildings' envelope is a black-coloured wood covering. The various grades used give a more random texture, referring to vernacular structures.

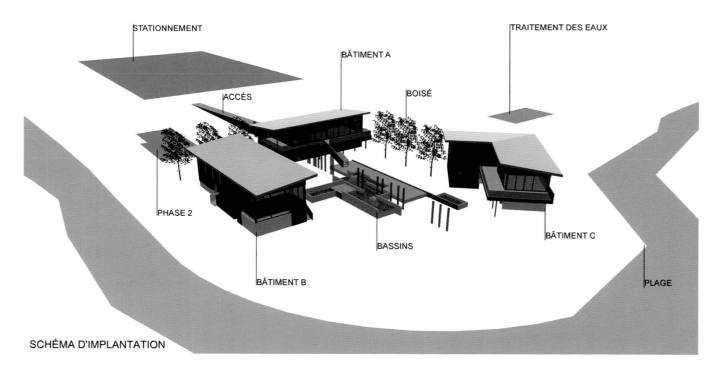

STATIONNEMENT

TRAITEMENT DES EAUX

BÂTIMENT A

ACCÈS

BOISÉ

PHASE 2

BÂTIMENT C

BASSINS

BÂTIMENT B

PLAGE

SCHÉMA D'IMPLANTATION

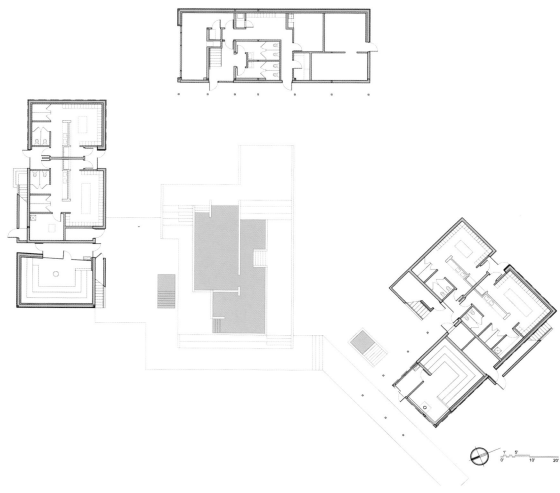

first floor plan

Once visitors enter the volume, the high ceilings and picture window project them into the exterior landscaping and the countryside.

A walkway is cut through the east wall of the main building; this is the only distinctive element marking the entrance to the project.

The interior spaces are uncluttered, giving the natural landscape the starring role. Bright colours are used only for specific elements, such as the restaurant's large banquette and the steam bath.

This resort has been widely considered as an excellent example of integrating well with its surroundings.

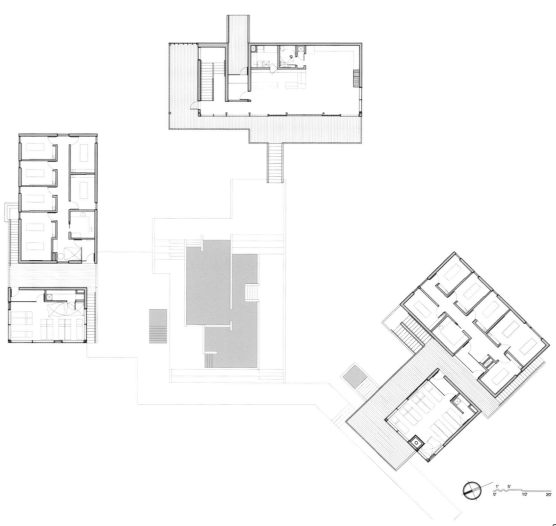

second floor plan

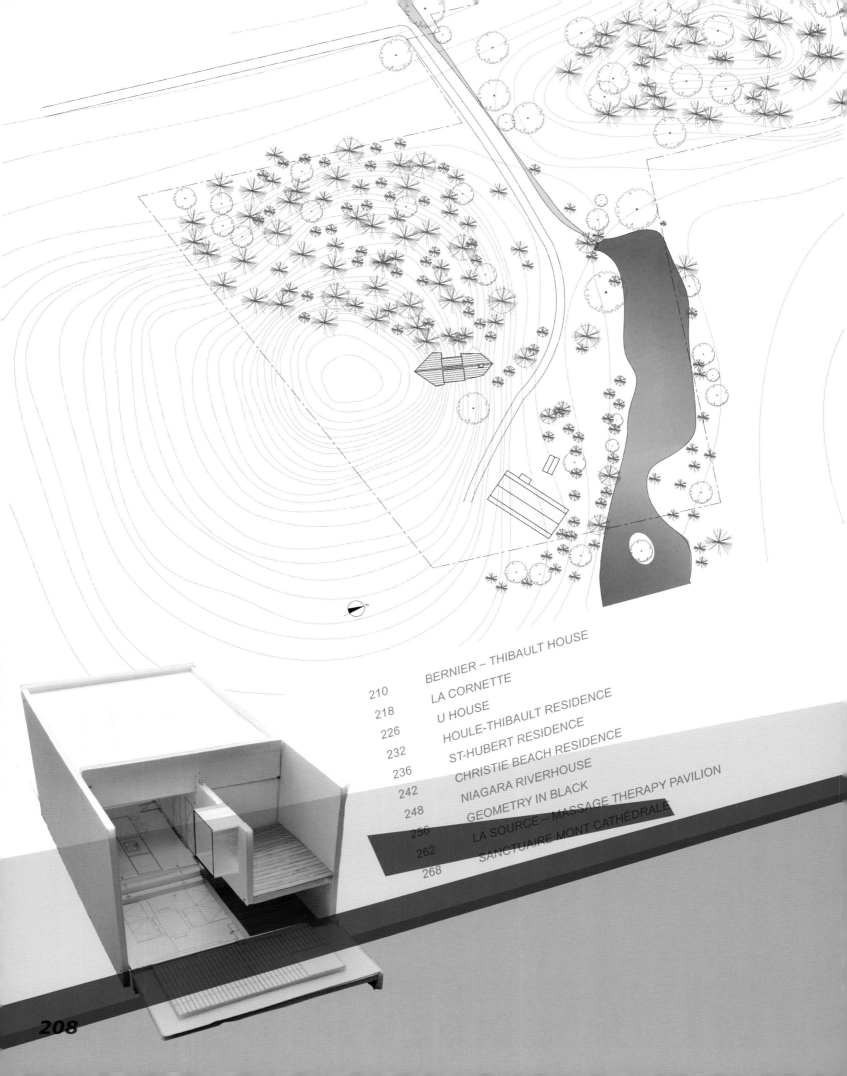

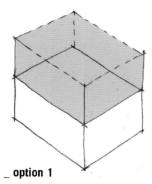

_ option 1

Adding a second floor into the
existing building:
inadequate foundation

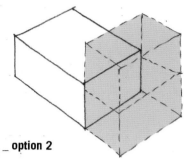

_ option 2

Two storey extension into the
backyard:
forbidden by the Municipality

_ option

backyard extension compressing the
spaces on numerous split-levels

RESIDENCE

Architect: Paul Bernier Architect

Location: Montreal, Quebec, Canada

Photographers: Marc Cramer, Paul Bernier, Vittorio Viera

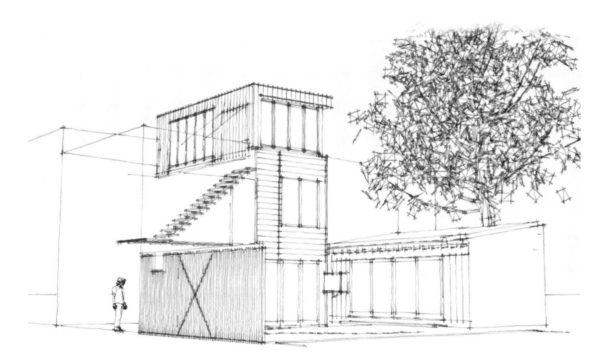

BERNIER – THIBAULT HOUSE

This extension and transformation of the house has to be made to allow for a family of four. Two rooms have to be added, one for the kids and one for the adults. Besides, the designers extend the house and preserve the quality of the garden while working to increase natural light. The house aims to become a perfect integral of the families' spirit and materiality.

Two boxes made of glass and wood, simple volumes of similar dimensions, are added to the original house. One box is placed on the roof and the other one in the garden under the big maple. A vertical slice of the original garden side wall was taken out and replaced by a wood structure wall that allows for openings on the garden and that acts as a formal link between the two boxes.

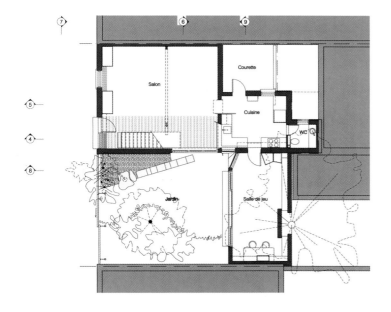

first floor plan

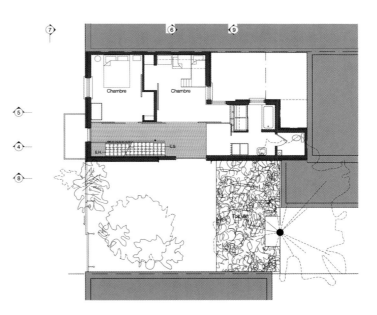

second floor plan

The box on the roof shelters the adult room, like a big hat. Standing on it, people can see the city and the sunrise. The box also smoothly leads the natural light into the inside.

The box in the garden, a playroom for the children, is connected to the interior living spaces and opens up on the courtyard with wide glass doors as a pavilion in a garden, bright and transparent.

In addition, the ground floor, which serves as the space for family life, is an L-shape that, in the three sides, wraps around the garden and opens to the outside on one side, becoming an extra room in the summer, without any depressed feelings or darkness.

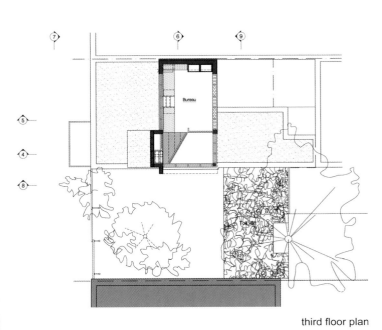

third floor plan

217

Architect: YH2-Yiaconvalicis Hamelin Architects

Builder: Emmanuel Yiacouvakis

Project Team: Marie-Claude Hamelin, Loukas Yiacouvakis

Location: Township of Cleveland, Quebec, Canada

Area: about 280 m²

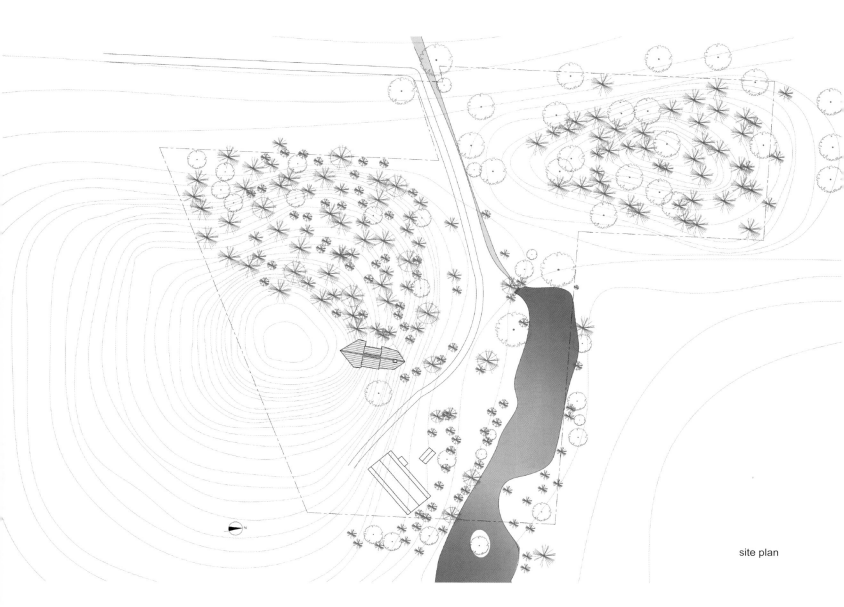

site plan

LA CORNETTE

Built on the slope of a small hill, La Cornette is a country house open to the pastoral landscape that surrounds it. This house for celebrations and holidays, designed for two families, is set into the naturally uneven terrain in a way that brings each level into direct contact with the surrounding natural environment. It offers a resting place for all guests under its large gable in a series of bedrooms and unusual sleeping areas.

An out-scaled structure, like the agricultural buildings that surround it, the house is both traditional in its morphology and innovative in its use of materials. Shingled with raw fibre-cement panels on the walls and roof, it is a house beyond the domestic scale, simple and rot-proof, capable of standing the test of time. The house is striated with bands of horizontal windows, giant louvers that cut the sun at its most powerful, with new points of view at each level. It is protected by its wimple from the hot summer sun and inundated with light in the winter, needing neither air-conditioning nor heating on sunny days.

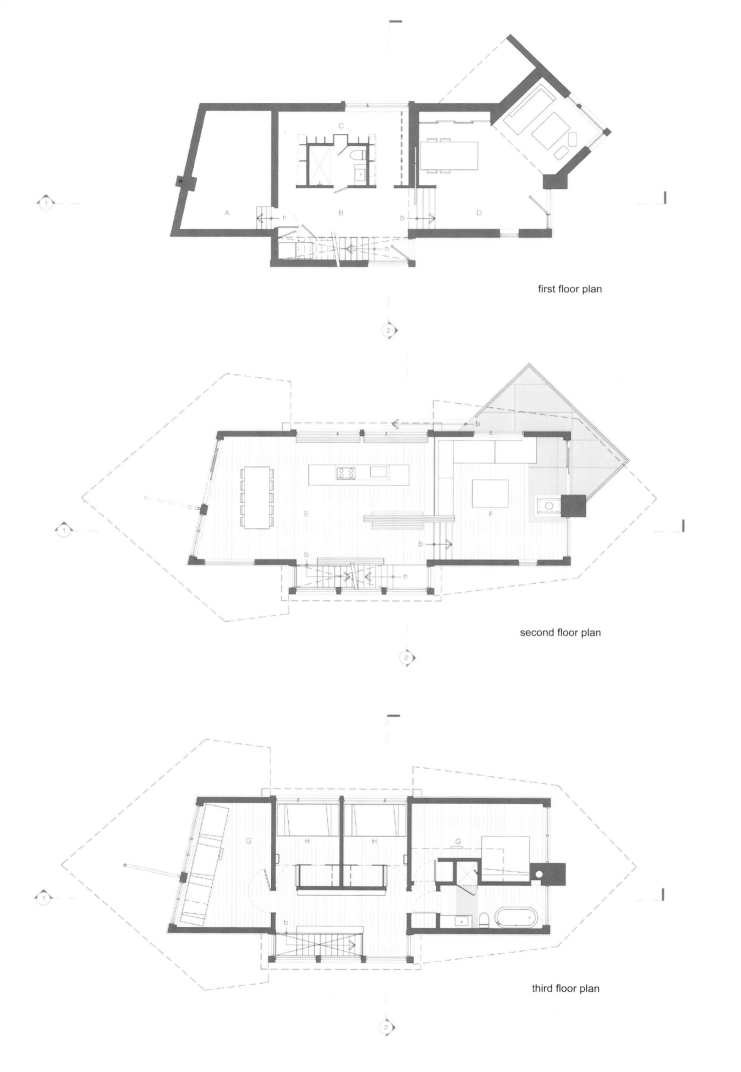

first floor plan

second floor plan

third floor plan

east elevation

south elevation

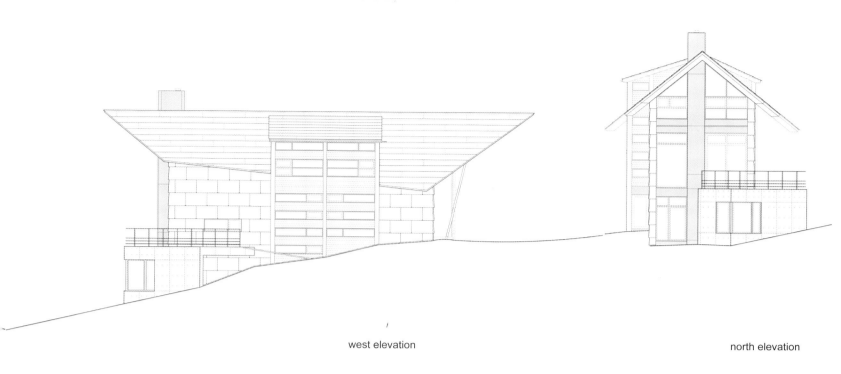

west elevation

north elevation

223

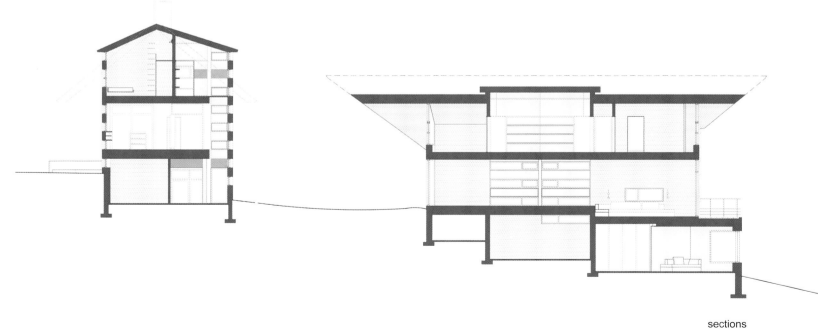

sections

The interior is in wood, painted or natural, in planks or panels, composed almost exclusively of made-to-measure furniture pieces, such as the refectory table for meals, the large wrap-around couch, the balustrade bookshelf along the stairway, the night-lights made of aluminum panels with cut-outs of fireflies, fish, and frogs; comfortable beds.

It is a playground for architects, children and adults, as well as a vacation colony lost in the countryside.

Architect: Natalie Dionne

Photographer: Marc Cramer

U HOUSE

Situated near a railway line on the outskirts of a trendy Montreal neighbourhood, the design of U House responds to a harsh urban context, respectfully shutting out the outside world by concentrating services around the periphery and creatively keeping away from the noisy outside world. Constructed with the precision of fine cabinetry, the articulated panels of wood, glass and steel that line the courtyard open and close to invite the outside in and the inside out.

U House was designed by architect Natalie Dionne to house both the family residence and her office space. She exploits the idea of fluidity between interior and exterior spaces. The Ipê wood deck which is an extension of the dining room's inlaid wood floor helps to confound the boundary between inside and outside when the large accordion style door is opened. At the other end of the L-shaped deck, one of the original building's huge French windows is actually a garage door that also opens up fully to seamlessly integrate the living room with the garden. For added spatial continuity and a layered effect, the wood and steel façade elements of the new additions were mapped to the interior.

Doors and windows of Cedro wood, marine plywood panels and cedar bifold shutters are all stained for uniformity and mimic the color of the brick on the original building, creating a brand-new look.

The shutters upstairs are opened. This ensures sufficient ventilation, guarantees privacy, protects from the rain, and keeps the south-facing rooms nicely cool. What deserves to mention is that in summer, at night, whether it is raining heavily outside or not, it is always quiet and comfortable. What a pleasant resort!

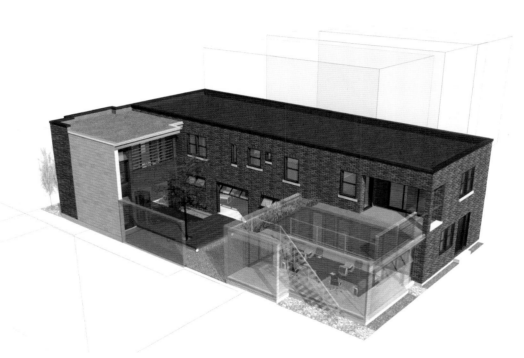

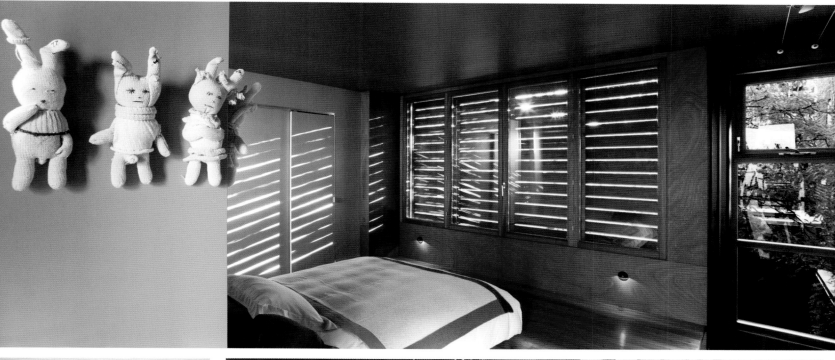

Architect: Chevalier Morales Architect

Project Managers: Sergio Morales, Stephan Chevalier

Project Team: Sergio Morales, Stephan Chevalier, Karine Dieujuste, Christine Giguère, Samantha Hayes

Location: Mont-Tremblant, Quebec, Canada

Site Area: 4,500 m²

Built Area: 300 m²

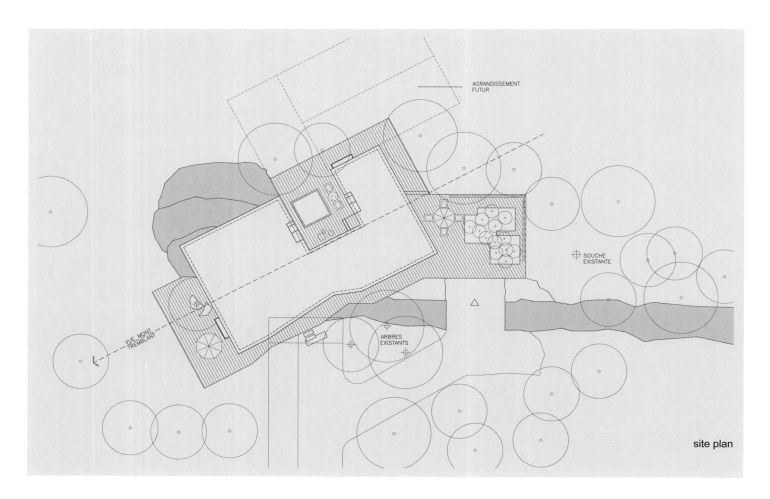

AGRANDISSEMENT
FUTUR

SOUCHE
EXISTANTE

VUE MONT
TREMBLANT

ARBRES
EXISTANTS

site plan

HOULE-THIBAULT RESIDENCE

Built on a mountainside with incredible views of Tremblant Montain, the Houle-ThibanIt Residerce embodies a sense of obvious nostalgia of traditional architecture, as well as tastes old and exquisite qualities in natural areas.

Following the client's initial request to have a timber-framed house, the designers worked with the help of a local artisan and after multiple iterations of the frame, they ended up not only achieving the simplest possible shape but we also managed to dissimulate all anchorage so the frame could be read without the interference of steel plates and bolts.

The residence sits silently on a rock vein, as if it had emerged naturally from the landscape. The mineral base contains the garage, storage and technical spaces

When entering the residence, in a double-height space, a set of four large windows allows an immediate view of the top of the trees. On both south and west sides, the shape retracts itself on the ground floor, creating an integrated pare-soleil that helps maintain these windowed spaces shaded during the summer.

The residence is full of recreational and natural fragrance, small and lovely.

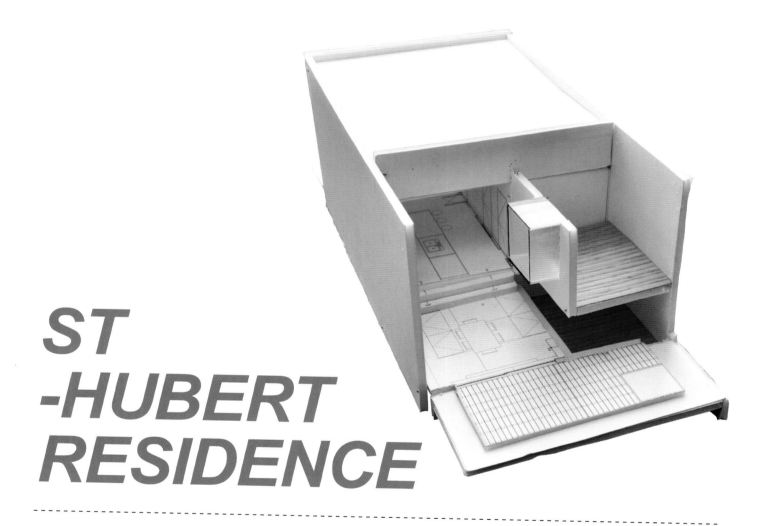

ST -HUBERT RESIDENCE

The clients wished to enlarge their 74 m² bungalow by adding a second floor to the existing structure. However, the poor conditions of the foundations quickly proved this option impossible. In turn, the architects studied the possibility to build an extension into the backyard. Two major constraints were to be found: 1. the Municipality forbades constructing higher than the existing roof membrane, 2. the presence of the 1-meter rock into the ground made the construction of a basement very costly. From those limitations, an unconventional and affordable solution was developed: compressing the spaces on numerous split-levels to yield the desired rooms, with a stunning double-height dining room and a generous provision of natural light.

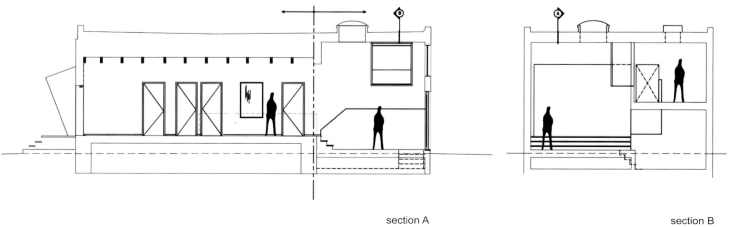

section A   section B

The first gesture was to lower the new dining room to the level of the exterior terrace and to link it with the kitchen and music room through a vast open space. Suspended atop the dining room, a translucent reading cube emerges from the master bedroom, creating a quiet and comfortable reading space. The kitchen is organized around an over-dimensioned central counter that becomes the focus of the social life in the house.

To meet the extremely tight budget, the selected building materials were deliberately left raw and untouched. The floor is covered mostly with an antic waxed maple flooring while the dining room uses fibrocement panels. The roof structure of the existing house was left exposed and painted in white to lighten up the spaces. The exterior back facade is covered with black pine planks with industrial corrugated steel sheet with galvalum finish.

Playing in a subversive manner with the numerous constraints, the architects yielded a unique project. Simple and modest, St-Hubert residence offers nonetheless a rich spatial experience with generous and luminous spaces.

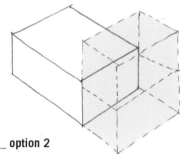

_ **option 2**

Two storey extension into the
backyard:
forbidden by the Municipality

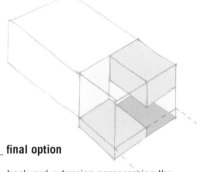

_ **final option**

backyard extension compressing the
spaces on numerous split-levels

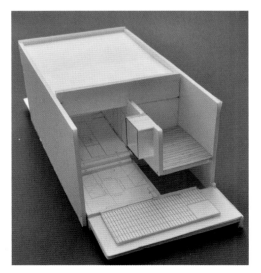

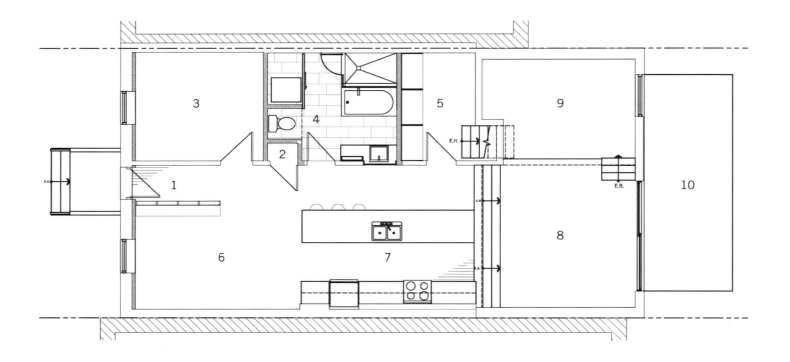

1. hall	3. bedroom	5. walk-in	7. kitchen	9. living room	
2. cloakroom	4. bathroom	6. music room	8. dinning room	10. exterior terrace	first floor plan

Architect: Altius Architecture Inc.

Leading Design Architect: Graham Smith

Location: Christie Beach, Ontario, Canada

Area: 557 m²

CHRISTIE BEACH RESIDENCE

Set on the south shore of Georgian Bay, this residence seeks to harmonize with its surrounding landscape with a minimal environmental impact while accommodating the diverse needs of four generations of occupants. Integration with the site is achieved by setting the building low and shifting floor and roof planes so that it becomes embed into the landscape. As the elevations shifts between the deck, loft, upper patio, green roof and floor levels; intimate moments are created as each space unfolds distinctly into the external environment. The elevation of the reflecting pool is also set specifically to create an effect of seamlessly extending Georgian Bay to the house, blurring the lines between building and landscape Material choice is also significant in addressing the issues of site responsiveness, sustainability and for comfort. The rich wood in of the interior spaces brings warmth to the spaces in winter while the rich red cedar and cherry woods intensify the vibrant green of the surrounding forest in summer. The exterior Ipe naturally blends with the surrounding rock soil, and becomes a geometric topography that extends its contemporary aesthetic into the natural environment.

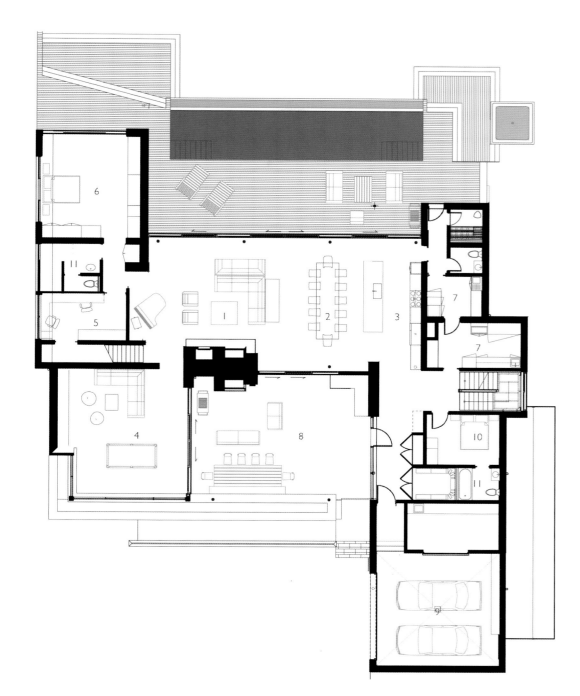

1. living
2. dining
3. kitchen
4. recreation
5. study
6. master bedroom
7. service
8. courtyard
9. garage

first floor plan

Flanked by hard edges on the east and west, the building maintains privacy from neighbours while emphasizing the views to the inner courtyard. The organization of the building is broken down into zones; the main floor is divided between the public / living area and service while upstairs there are the two wings – one for the master suite and the other for the guest wing to accommodate extended family. These spaces are unified by a central courtyard, which acts as the hub of the house, which gives access to all main spaces on the ground floor.

The building has plenty of sunlight. The continuous clerestory windows in the main pavilion offer daylight as well as a 360° view of the adjacent external environment while its upward sloping roof utilizes stack effect ventilation.

The building implements a ground-loop geothermal system as the primary heating system. Comprehensive sustainable technologies and building practice sets this project apart from others in the Blue Mountain region while the unique building form and functional program promise to provide a wonderful family retreat as well as a year round dwelling for its owners.

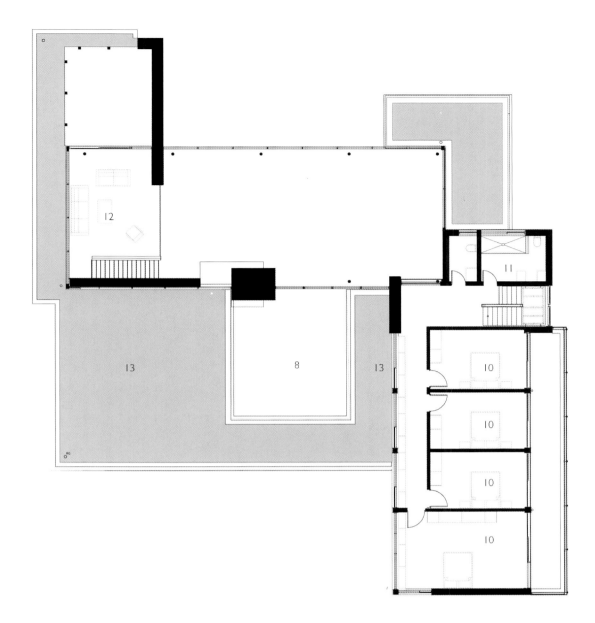

1. bedroom
2. WC
3. loft
4. green roof

second floor plan

Architect: Zerafa Studio Llc.

Location: Niagara Falls, Ontario, Canada

Site Area: 7,400 m²

Gross Floor Area: 500 m²

Photographer: Tom Arban

NIAGARA RIVERHOUSE

The house is comprised of three distinct horizontal volumes, each with a specific material quality. The building's north south massing is defined by two overlaid rectangular shells within which the glass, cedar and granite clad volumes for the interior living spaces are placed and a series of remaining voids create covered exterior spaces. The shell exteriors are clad in silver metal panel and are mostly opaque to provide privacy from adjacent properties to the north and south. The ground floor is comprised of two primary program groups separated by an east west glazed circulation space that bisects the house and extends the river views through to the rear garden.

The service and ancillary spaces, garage, storage, guest suite and access to the basement level are contained within a single-storey bar that runs east to west to minimize the obstruction of views. The primary living spaces are distributed in a linear bar across the width of the site to maximize exposure to river views. The home office, kitchen and dining room and double-height living room extend the full width of the north-south bar to mediate the front and rear gardens and establish a strong visual connection to the outdoors.

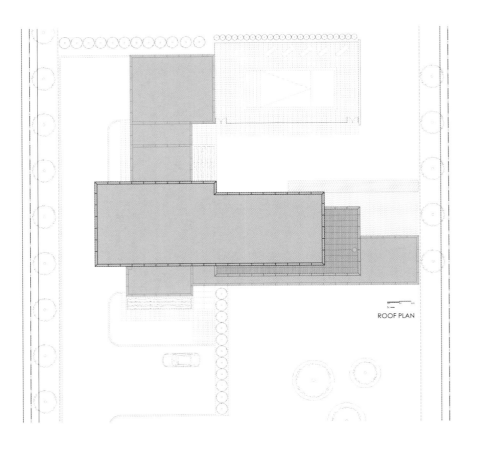

roof plan

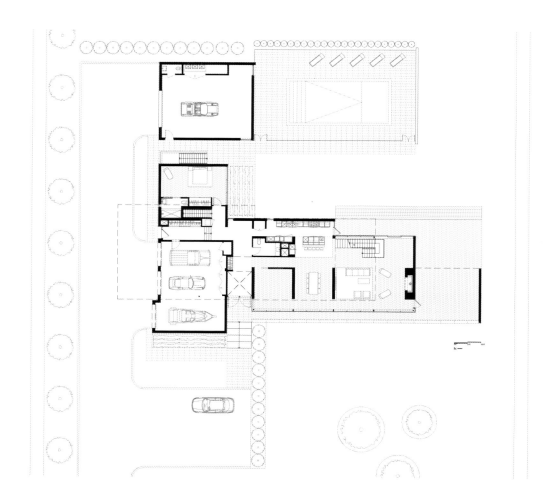

first floor plan

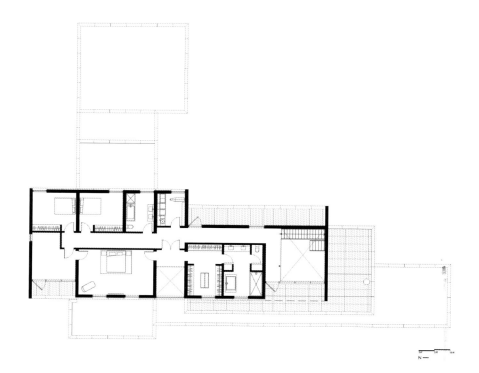

second floor plan

252

The more private spaces including an expansive master room, two additional bedrooms with en-suite bath and laundry facilities are distributed in a parallel bar on the second floor accessible by a dramatic sculptural stair. The master room extends the length of the river view façade, bridging across the circulation space below and extending out to a large covered terrace. The double-height living room features a custom-designed stair, engineered and fabricated locally of steel-reinforced maple, which is full of old and elegant fragrance of musuem.

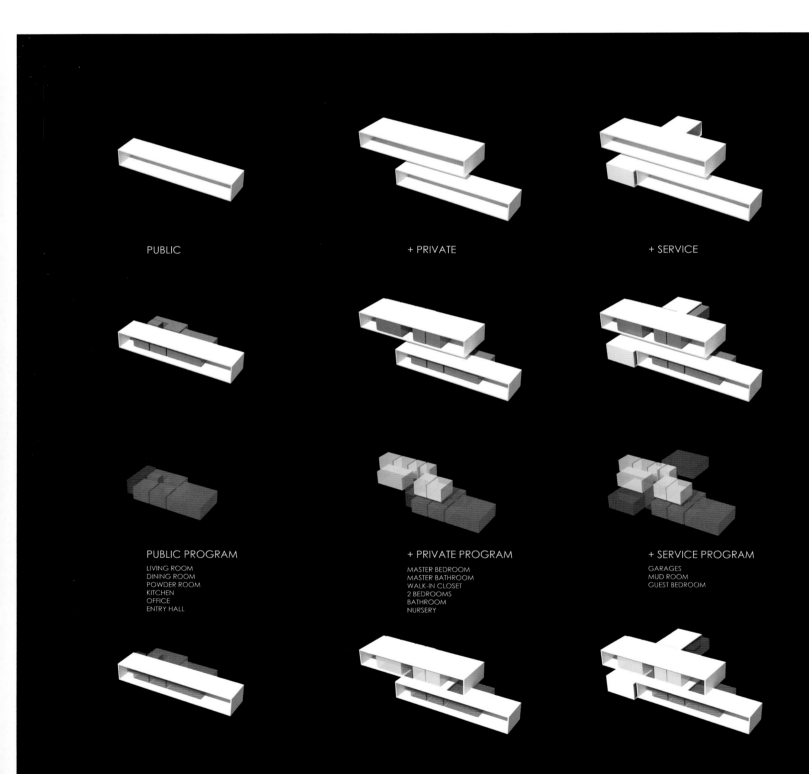

PUBLIC

+ PRIVATE

+ SERVICE

PUBLIC PROGRAM

LIVING ROOM
DINING ROOM
POWDER ROOM
KITCHEN
OFFICE
ENTRY HALL

+ PRIVATE PROGRAM

MASTER BEDROOM
MASTER BATHROOM
WALK-IN CLOSET
2 BEDROOMS
BATHROOM
NURSERY

+ SERVICE PROGRAM

GARAGES
MUD ROOM
GUEST BEDROOM

Architect: YH2_Yiacouvakis Hamelin Architects

Builder: Martin Lachance

Location: Saint-Hyppolite, Quebec, Canada

Project Team: Benoit Boivin, Marie-Claude Hamelin, Loukas Yiacouvakis

GEOMETRY IN BLACK

In the Laurentians, a dense forest on a slight hill, down-turns into the expansion of a small river. Through the trees, the body of a black building is divided into three blocks linked by glass passageways. Three blocks of a home, mid-level from each other, are all in direct contact with the earth. Three blocks of proper identity, offering intimacy between each and open to nature: An entry block, open on two levels and includes the adolescents quarters and family room. A daytime block, central space, friendly, opens onto the terrace. A private block, owners suite, isolated from the rest of the home.

On the north side of the house, a large section of bent corten steel with oblique lines connects the fragmented blocks together while defining a series of outdoor settings, always against the light. Partly-based in the geometric basis of the concept which dictates each project component, a sort of unwritten contract exists between architect and client. The modification of each element having a direct influence on the others, the work of enlarging or reducing a block in height and plan cannot be achieved without enlarging or reducing other areas of the house.

This geometry which is both fragmented and linear makes the project a strong spatial experience, allowing direct and variable contact with the landscape. It is this angular part, made of dark and raw materials that unites the house to nature, like a rock that emerges from the ground, or a forgotten shipwreck at the heart of the forest.

Architect: Blouin Tardif Architecture-Environnement

Landscape Architect: Projet Paysage

Structural Engineer: CLA Experts Conseils

Project Manager: Alexandre Blouin

Project Team: Isabelle Beauchamp, Sophie Martel, Jonathan Trottier, Alexandre Blouin

Location: Rawdon, Quebec, Canada

Photographer: Steve Montpetit

LA SOURCE – MASSAGE THERAPY PAVILION

This new pavilion is part of a resort grouping built on a mountainside in the Lanaudière region. The project as a whole is integrated into nature through its siting, the use of natural materials, and the framing of the surrounding landscape through generous openings in the contemporary architectural structure.

The construction of this building with an area of 800 m² has three levels. The facilities now include thirteen massage spaces and two new lounges. In addition, the new pavilion integrates a reception area for customers and administration offices. This combination of functions, requiring both a contemplative ambience and a workplace, represented not only one of the challenges for the project but also the most significant concern to the designer.

The project is designed as a procession featuring the surrounding natural environment. Visitors arrive at the pavilion via a long wooden walkway overlooking the forest. This outdoor passageway leads to the entrance while establishing a dialogue with the adjacent escarpment. Situated in the centre of the building and framed by rough-concrete walls, the main stairway provides access to all levels.

The building's cladding is made of torrefacted poplar; torrefaction is a procedure that makes the material (a local wood species) very strong and durable.

264

The green L-shaped concrete roof orients the pavilion toward the mountain and the forest. The roof, like a big umbrella, protects the building envelopes, the fenestration, outdoor walkways, and the patio. It has been polished and left visible to minimize finishes and maximize the thermal mass effect. The radiant-floor heating system is deployed in all spaces, providing comfortable, efficient warmth to users.

This project is intended first and foremost to be a space of relaxation and contemplation in the midst of nature. It integrates the values proposed during the design process: the comfort of the occupants through the use of warm, natural materials with simple forms, contact with the surrounding landscape, and a structure in harmony with nature.

Architect: Pierre Cabana

Location: Brompton, Quebec, Canada

Photographer: Richard Poissant et Pierre Léveillé

SANCTUAIRE MONT CATHÉDRALE

The house uses art as much as architecture to blend into its surroundings. Inspired by a tree, the house's first floor is covered in wood to represent a tree trunk. The much larger second floor is covered in copper tiles (leaves), which will, in time, develop a green patina, helping the house harmonize with the surrounding vegetation. An immense glass wall faces southeast on the front of the house and opens onto a 70 m² terrace looking out onto a panoramic view of the lake and neighboring mountains. The terrace is 54 m above lake level, creating a sense of weightlessness and direct contact with the natural elements.

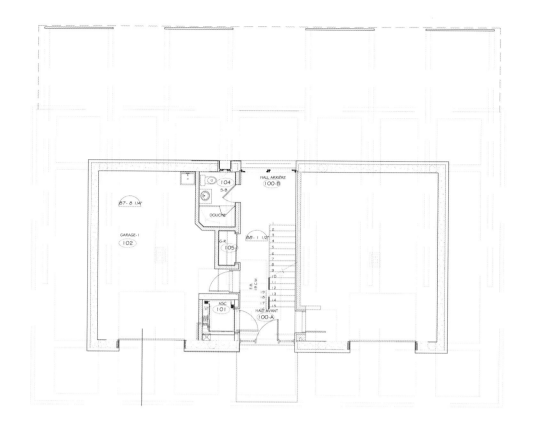

first floor plan

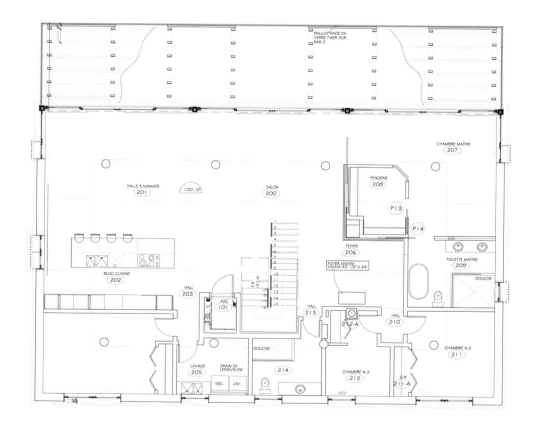

second floor plan

270

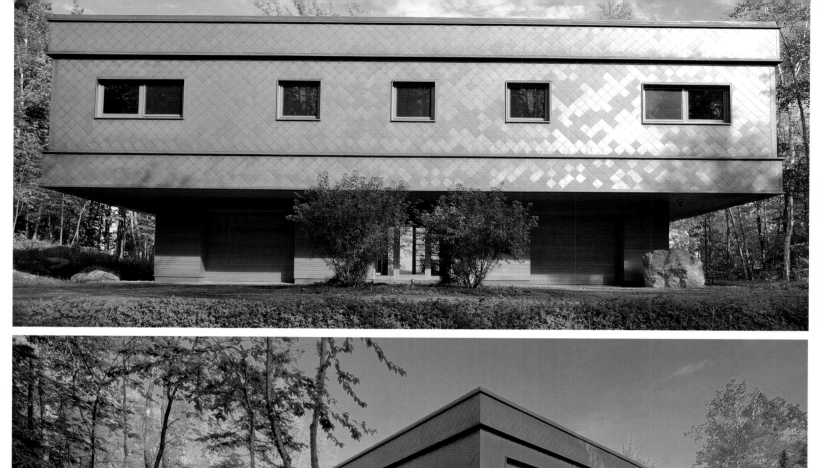

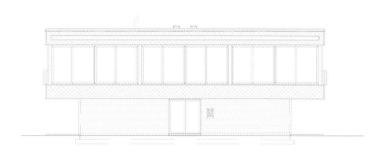

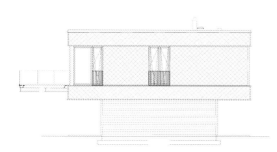

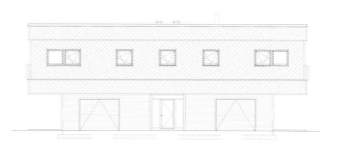

Inside, the house is friendly and warm thanks to the judicious use of natural and manufactured materials. The marriage of wood, marble, quartz, steel, glass, and porcelain creates a harmonious connection with the natural environment.

Insulated with great care, the house has excellent energy efficiency. The heating system uses a combination of geothermal energy. In addition, the glass wall increases the energy efficiency of the house. In winter, sunlight comes in and reduces heating costs; in summer, electric, automatic awnings keep the interior cool.

RUE SAINT-JACQUES

RUE GAUVIN

RUE MC GILL

RUE NOTRE-DAME

OFFICE

SUGAR CUBE

This mixed-use development project introduces a new strategy for making contemporary architecture within Denver's historic Lower Downtown Heritage District (LoDo).

The client's specific functional and performance goals included building for longevity as a form of sustainability, achieving cost savings with energy efficient systems and enduring design, and creating an active street-related base to contribute to the revitalization of the district.

The project is located on the 16th Street Mall, a major public pedestrian thoroughfare that runs through the city of Denver. The building features a central ten-storey volume in manganese-colored brick, wrapped around by buff brick. The top of the parapet of Sugar Cube is set at a height that aligns with the underside of the upper cornice of the Sugar Building. The roof provides generous and bright outdoor terraces to show the beauty of the whole city.

The darkness of the cube's brick and the way it interacts with Denver's strong light creates a dramatic contrast with the lighter masonry volumes, and inserts an iconic, modernist form on the Denver skyline. The scheme explores alternatives to conventional balconies associated with residential developments to create drawer-like projections from the building, and make an unusual interplay of form against Denver's brilliant blue skies and distant views of the Rocky Mountains.

site plan

HEAD OFFICE OF QUEBECOR

At the crossroads of Old Montreal and the Quartier international de Montréal, Quebecor's new head office is set in an architectural context punctuated by different eras. limestone-clad base blends with the horizontality of Rue Notre-Dame, topped by a glass-wall tower that dialogues with the adjacent towers, and the twenty-one-storey building is harmoniously wedded with a dense and relatively complex urban fabric. Seen from Victoria Square, the tower's sharp, atypical silhouette matches the urban landscape.

The present project involves an expansion of 170,000 m², with the south side abutting the existing 13-storey building by an internal passageway.

As a natural continuity with the existing building, three conditions seemed essential to the architects: How to connect the two buildings to the urban context and environment in every sense? How to adopt refined approaches to urban design and project management? How to achieve the client's needs of an economical, simple project in a context of performance and long-term value, based on the high-quality materials?

284

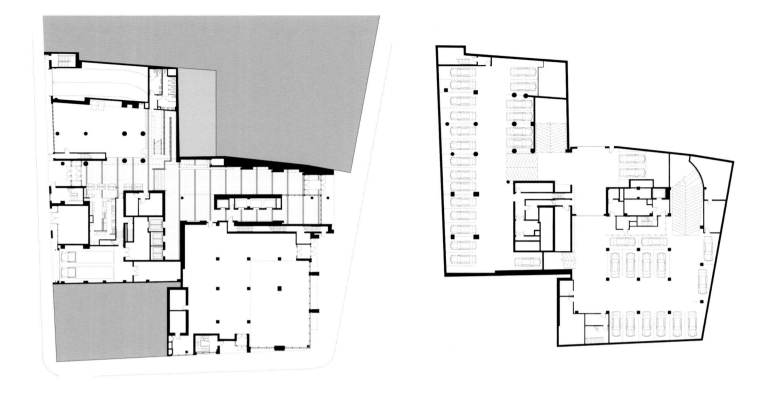

Therefore, the idea of making full use of the structure of the existing building by grafting a second building in continuity with it was the beginning of a long series of principles that led the architects to think about their project around the concepts of recycling and reinterpretation of the existing architectural elements. This dynamic of linking the two projects is very perceptible in the color and texture of the façades, in which volumes of glass and masonry stretch vertically, meeting or extending to the top. Limestone, black granite, glass and aluminum are used to create a neutral-colored building alliance.

The architect has introduced a number of green roofs with sharp forms, enclosing a small garden. They effectively reduce the heat-island effect retain rainwater, improves the lifespan of the waterproofing membranes, and encourages biodiversity with diverse flowers and trees. Although the idea was set aside due to budgetary constraints, it remained with the owner, who finally gave it the go-ahead as the project was being completed.

On the ground floor, the creation of a new entrance hall takes advantage of the relocation of the old parking-access ramp. Thus, a new two-storey-high public passageway crosses the two buildings from one side to the other, connecting Rue Notre-Dame to Victoria Square. In its centre, a reception area formed of a long furniture wall of black granite faced with glass directs the public toward the vertical circulation and services spaces, creating a sense of horizontality, transparency and airiness.

All of the interior spaces in the project are designed, from the beginning, as obstacle-free and universally accessible environments, with a lot of service infrastructure convenient for the disabled. Benefiting from the greatest autonomy possible, complete freedom and safety will be enjoyed.

Quebecor's new head office respects a defined urban architecture style, innovative, functional and tasteful.

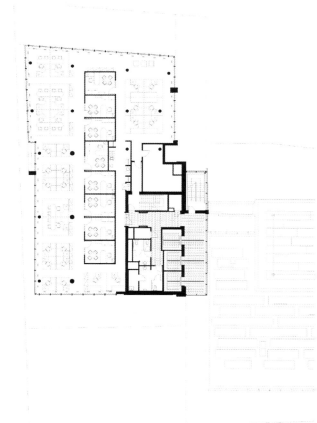

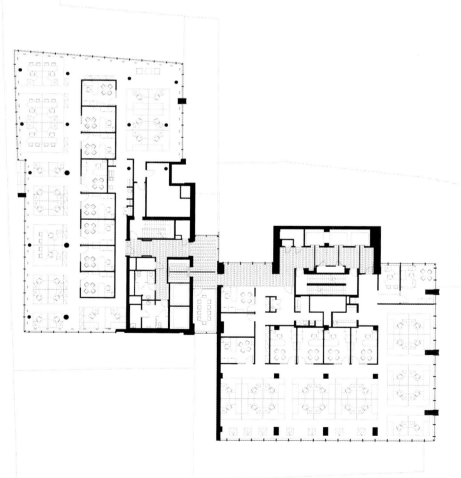

Architect: WZMH Architects

Landscape Architect: Dillon Consulting

Interior Architect of Base Building: WZMH Architects

Structural Engineer: Halcrow Yolles

Location: Toronto, Ontario, Canada

Area: 111, 000 m²

Photographer: Tom Arban

BAY ADELAIDE CENTRE TOWER

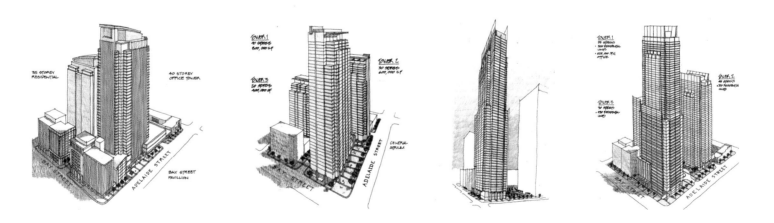

The 51-storey Bay Adelaide Centre Tower, completed in January 2010, is located on the western edge of a development site that occupies two city blocks, in the financial core of the City of Toronto. The project contains over 111,000 m² of rentable class-AAA office space and includes over 3,700 m² of below-grade retail space linked to the downtown's path system.

At the corner of Bay Adelaide Street, the highly transparent main building lobby, with walls clad in classic Statuario marble and Makore wood, engages passersby. At night, the illuminated lobby becomes a "beacon" at the corner of Bay and Adelaide Streets.

The project is a modernist building inspired by and paying homage to, the distinctive character of the architecture of Toronto's Financial Core. More transparent than any other in the downtown, the tower is a pristine glass prism clad in clear vision glass and spandrel panels with ceramic frit. The glazing is supported by four sided structural silicone within a channel surround creating a sense of lightness and delicacy for the building skin.

At the top of the tower, the curtain wall extends beyond the roof to become a series of "sails" that create a distinctive silhouette on the city skyline.

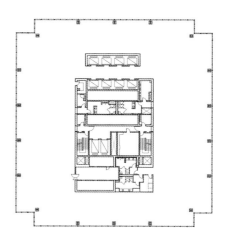

typical plan

294

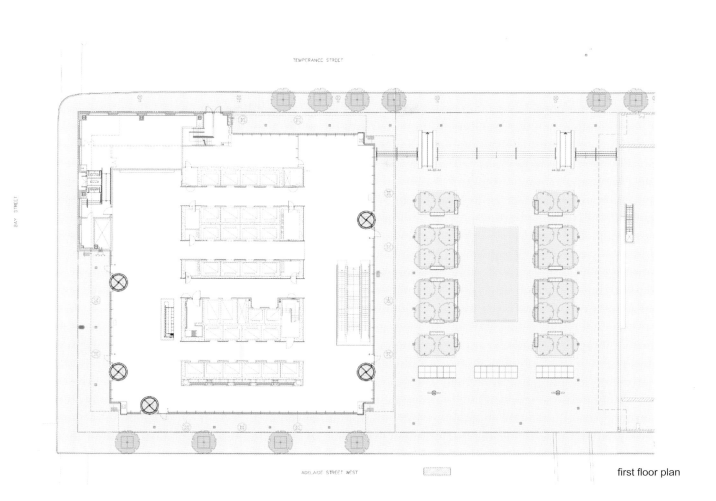

TEMPERANCE STREET

BAY STREET

ADELAIDE STREET WEST

first floor plan

The floors and the plaza are clad in a "carpet" of Brazilian Ipanema granite expressing a modernist sensibility for spatial continuity from inside to out.

Respecting the formality of the tower the plaza's design is simple, comprised of a central lawn framed by planting beds of natural grasses with two double rows of Ginko trees and comfortable seating benches.

The project provides flexible and cost-effective design model, emphasizes energy conservation, and follows sustainable principle. It successfully creates a secure, efficient and comfortable working environment.

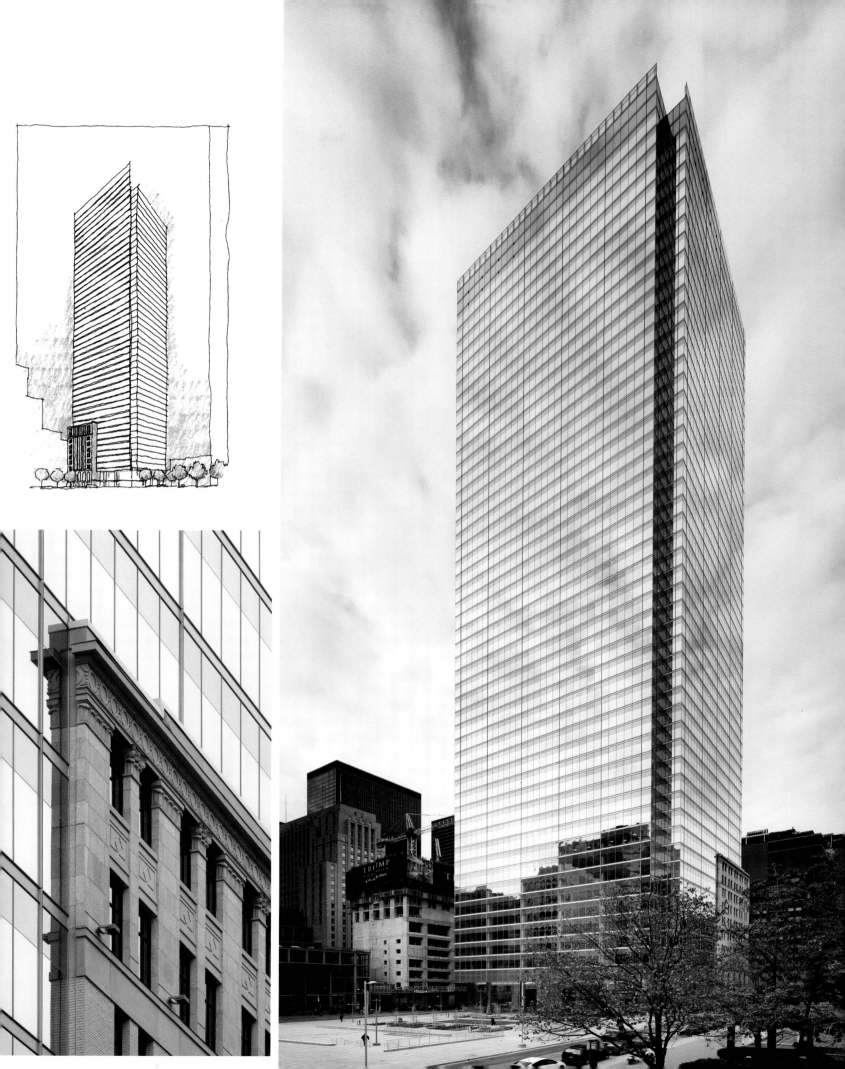

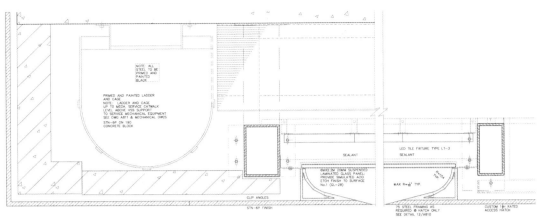

PUBLIC ART— PLAN DETAIL

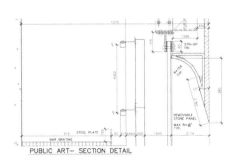

PUBLIC ART— SECTION DETAIL

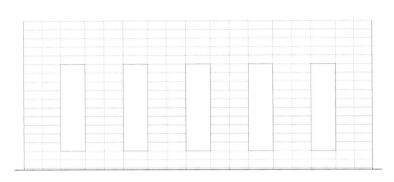

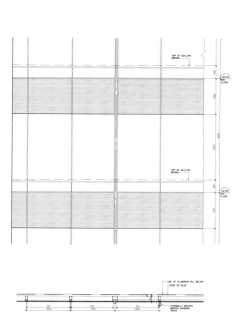

curtain wall detail

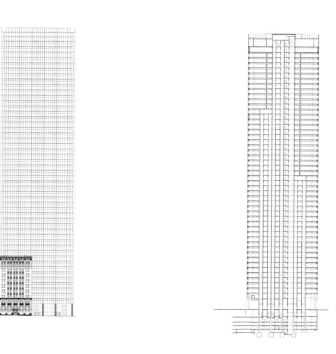

west elevation

north-south section

Architect: WZMH Architects

Landscape Architect: Gordon Ratcliffe Landscape Architects

Structural Engineer: BMR Structural Engineering

Location: Halifax, Nova Scotia, Canada

Area: 17,930 m²

Photographer: RPM Productions

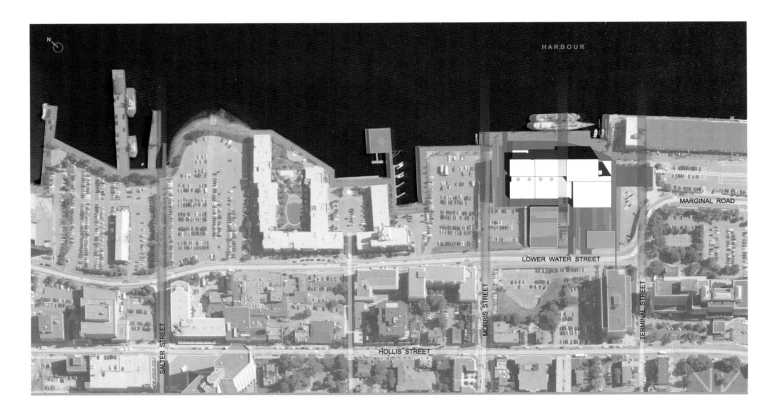

NOVA SCOTIA POWER INC.

The project is located on a 5-acre site at the southern end of the Halifax downtown waterfront with access from Lower Water Street. The site steps down approximately 7.5 meters from Lower Water Street to the harbor, east of the site. To the south, there has been significant redevelopment of some of existing harbor buildings. To the north and west, vacant lots exist that will be subject to future development.

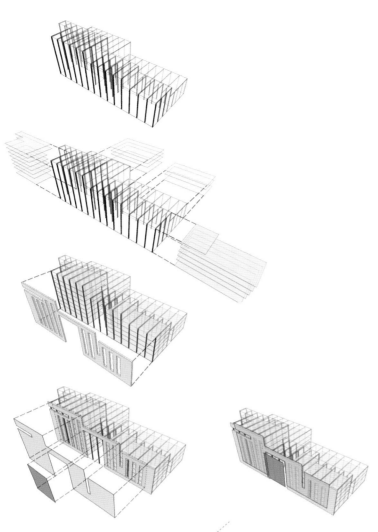

The project involves the retention and adaptive reuse of the former generating plant to become the headquarters for the provincial electrical utility, Nova Scotia Power Inc. (NSPI). The facility will house over 500 staff in approximately 18,000 gross m² and provide onsite parking for 150 cars.

Early visits to the site were inspirational: soaring interior spaces with an exposed latticework of steel framework were reminiscent of the imagery of Russian Deconstructivism design. Investigation of archival photos of the site uncovered the image of a line of 4 chimney stacks, becoming unique skylines.

As the provincial power authority, NSPI wishes to demonstrate environmental responsibility and show leadership in energy conservation. The unique adaptive reuse of the building will be a visible statement of the corporation's

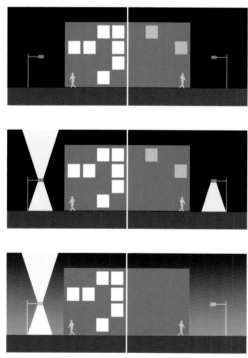

302

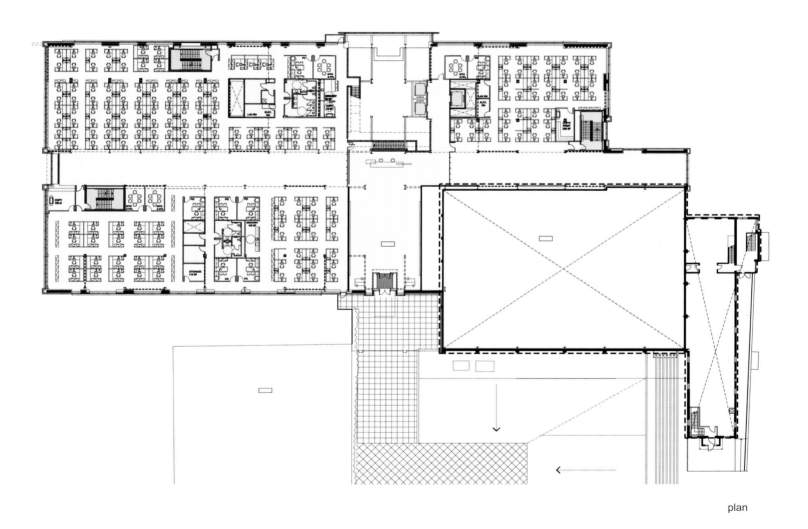

plan

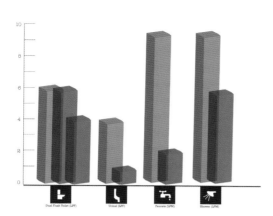

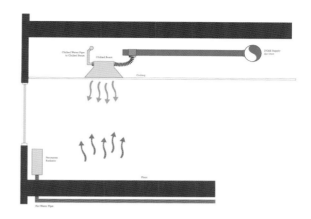

commitment to sustainability. Sea water cooling (and heating) is being provided utilizing existing piping from the Halifax harbor originally used to cool power generating turbines. The building will represent the first major use of "chilled beam" technology in Canada. Located within the ceiling space, the system, more efficient than conventional systems, utilizes (low energy sea) water rather than air to transport cooling thereby lowering energy consumption.

Additional energy saving strategies include the provision of heat recovery on HVAC, daylight and occupancy sensors for lighting and supplemental heating for both the building and hot water with the use of solar thermal panels. NSPI deserves to be the example model of the energy-saving industry.

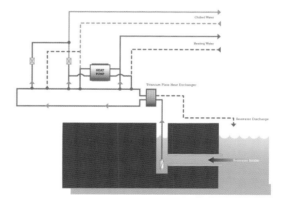

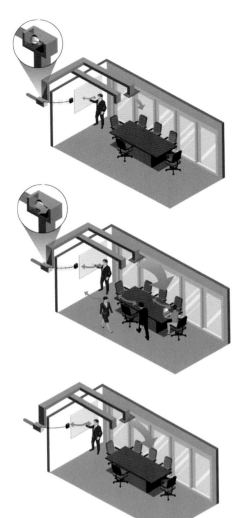

Architect: DCYSA Architecture & Design (Anh Lequang, Lucien Haddad, Azad Chichmanian)

Special Collaborator: Lyse M. Tremblay, PA LEED

Photographers: Gleb Gomberg, Alex St-Jean

SIÈGE SOCIAL DE SCHLÜTER-SYSTEMS INC.

Sustainability and design are interwoven in this industrial structure. Technology is celebrated and treated as an integral aesthetic experience. A medium-sized project in surface area, the building explodes with innovation and reads as a rigorous exercise in energy efficiency and contemporary language. The client is Schlüter-Systems, a company that manufactures accessories and membrane products centered on the tiling industry, and thrives on experimentation and perfection.

The building is the Canadian headquarters and serves as an office and training centre of the company's products. The two programs are architecturally distinct and

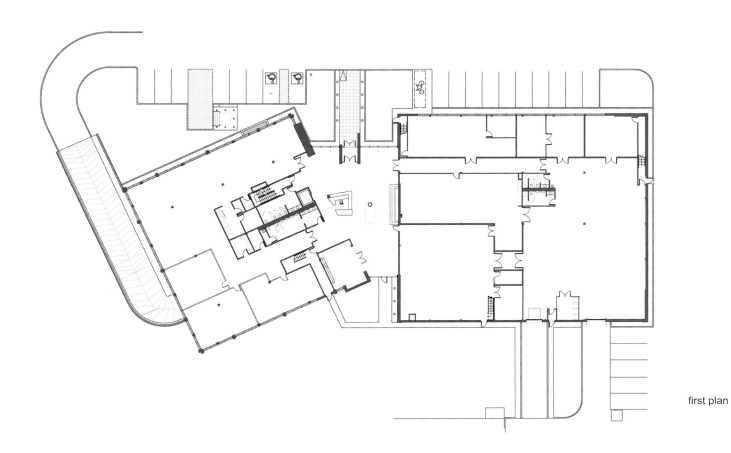

first plan

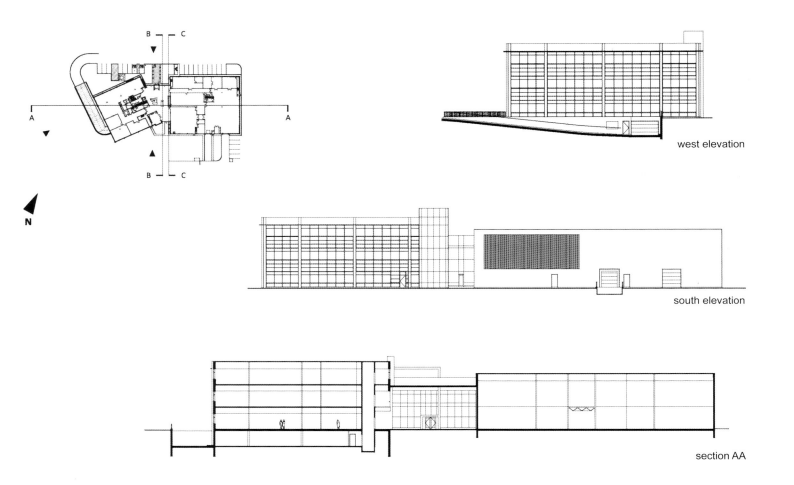

west elevation

south elevation

section AA

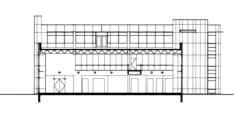

section BB

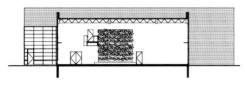

section CC

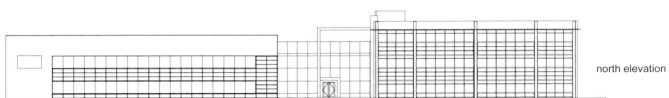

north elevation

connected by a delicate glass box, with a bold folded plane in the foreground marking the entrance. The combination of elements – towers, glass, folded plinth – reads as a harmonious exchange of lightness and depth, and points to the expertise of the company. The industrial complex is quiet and distinguished, sitting in a large wooded site in Sainte-Anne-de-Bellevue.

The combination of a dedicated team of specialists and an integrated process leads to a successful LEED-Gold certified building. Moving beyond basic principles of sustainability, the project manages to bring innovation to water management, energy use, and material selection. Ultimately, the building not only celebrates the company it was built for, it promises a long existence of pleasant use and ease of maintenance.

The building stands as a model for the possibilities of a successful business, and points to the future of environmentally intelligent corporate design directions.

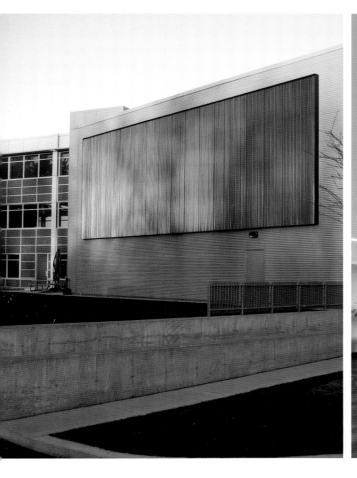

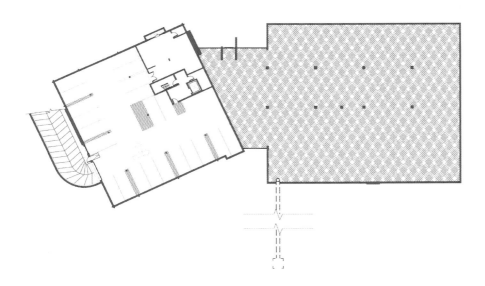

basement plan

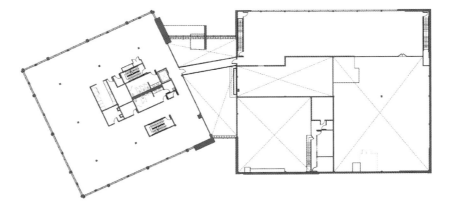

second plan

313

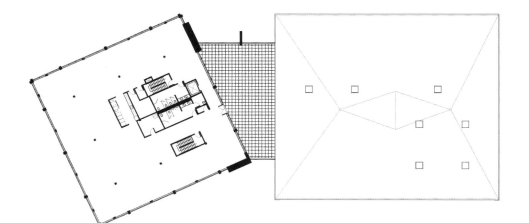

third plan

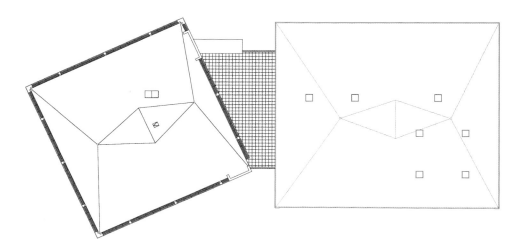

roof plan

Architect: LEMAY

Location: Montreal, Quebec, Canada

Area: 12,000 m²

Photographer: Claude-Simon Langlois

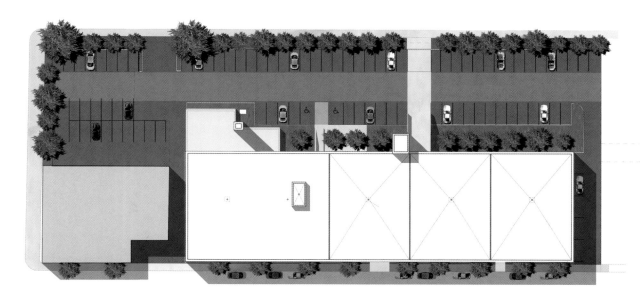

site plan

780 BREWSTER

780 Brewster is a five-storey multi-tenant industrial building with a total surface area of 12,000 m². This brick and timber building was transformed into an office building housing, elegant and exquisite.

What deserves to mention is that the structure meets the most rigorous sustainable development standards and is certified LEED Silver.

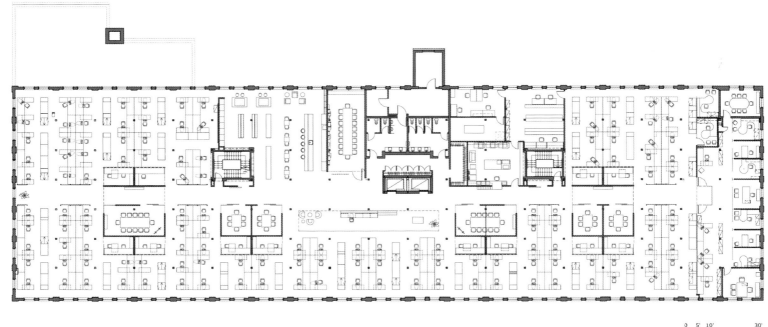

plan